Men, food, fellowship, and Jesus

BASECAMP

A 7-week Bible study for men seeking His will for them

TJ GREANEY *and*
JOE DON MAYES

KOZ PUBLISHING COMPANY

Austin, Texas

Cover photo: "Water Valley Cabin Night Campfire Alberta" copyright Philip Matejko, 2020. Used under license from Shutterstock.com.

Cover title box and art, chapter heading art, icon art derived from "Set of vintage outdoor camp badges and emblems" © Depositphotos.com/emberstock

Editing: Dana L. Cobb
Book Design: Tamara Dever, TLC Book Design, TLCBookDesign.com

ISBN: 978-0-9909924-5-5
ISBN: 978-0-9909924-6-2 (Audiobook)
ISBN: 978-0-9909924-7-9 (E-book)

First Edition

Printed in the United States.

CONTENTS

v

BASE CAMP:
The Trail to Becoming Who
You Long to Be (as a Real Man)

vii

WHERE IT STARTED
FOR THESE TWO
TRAILHANDS

1

INTRODUCTION
OF THE STORY
Meet TJ and Joe Don

7
Chapter 1
AS A YOUNG BOY:
The Journey Begins

21
Chapter 2
THE TEENAGE BOY
AND HIS JOURNEY

37
Chapter 3
THE YOUNG MAN TRAIL

53
Chapter 4
AS AN ADULT MAN

69
Chapter 5
RISING AS A
LEADER OF MEN

87
Chapter 6
SETTLING IN
WISDOM

97
Chapter 7
DESTINY IN AN
ENCOUNTER WITH JESUS

103
FACILITATOR
INSTRUCTIONS FOR
GROUP BIBLE STUDIES

107
RESOURCES FOR
GROWING STRONGER

BASE CAMP:
The Trail to Becoming Who You Long to Be (as a Real Man)

So often men are told if they are parking cars, passing the plate, or even being deacons or elders, they are doing what a good Christian man does. The reward is a pat on the back, a once a year volunteer luncheon, and a matching t-shirt or all-expense paid retreat. It is true that being a part of the church, a member, and a volunteer is an important and Biblical piece of our walk, but for most guys those rewards are bland, shallow, and cheesy. It surely does not give them a sense of mission that reaches deeply into their souls, one that gets them excited to mount up and fight a battle for Jesus.

> *"But a Christ who is all grace cannot stir the masculine soul. Deep down, men long for a harsh affection—the love of a coach who yells at his players to get every ounce of effort; the love of a drill sergeant who pushes his recruits to the limits of human endurance; the love of a teacher who demands the impossible from his students. As Western society feminizes, it's getting harder for men to find this kind of love. The Lion of Judah offers harsh father-love in abundance—yet he's becoming an endangered species in the modern church."*
> – David Murrow, *Why Men Hate Going to Church.*

Many men don't know they can fight until you train them. They don't know that they have the ability to do anything serious for Jesus until you show them that they do. When a man discovers his strengths and where God wants him, he can align his heart in battle and with a cause. Once he has experienced the Holy Spirit in his heart while fighting for Jesus, he will know what the purpose of his existence truly is.

> *"Battle is the most magnificent competition in which a human being can indulge. It brings out all that is best; it removes all that is base. All men are afraid in battle. The coward is the one who lets his fear overcome his sense of duty. Duty is the essence of manhood."*
> – George S. Patton

We as men must stand up, step in, and fight for our hearts, our wives, our families, our faith, our church. We must have a cause we believe in and a commitment to that cause so deep it drives us forward. To find it, we have to start at the beginning—our beginning. We have been trained along our life trail, all the good, the bad, the horrible, the amazing, the joyful, and the beautiful. All our life experiences from when we were little add up to today and the mission for which we are perfectly trained. In this study you will walk with two guys through what that lifetime of training looked like for them. We share our deepest hurts and our amazing encounters with Jesus. Two regular guys who did not set out looking for Jesus, but realized that He was there the whole time, waiting for the prodigal sons to come home.

Every guy needs something to dig into. If you take the time to go all the way through this book, our prayer is for you to be inspired, moved, provoked in your walk with Jesus and who He made you to be. Jesus chose the original 12; he has chosen you. We pray you find out that meaning or a deeper sense of who you are in him. Godspeed brothers. Mount up.

Next Step

Life is never meant to be lived alone. We recommend you go through this book, ride this trail, with a friend or even better a group of men. Your story will help other men discover the lessons of their own lives. We have included a **Facilitator's Guide** in the back of the book that will walk you through the next seven weeks on this trail.

WHERE IT STARTED FOR THESE TWO TRAILHANDS

Joe Don Flack Mayes and I (TJ Greaney) have been friends for over 10 years. Joe Don was my pastor for many of those years as I was learning how to ride a new trail, one with Jesus leading. The first time we met was in a Wednesday morning Bible study for men. It was the usual early morning men's study common in churches across America. Joe Don was new to the area and to the small Bible church I went to that met in the high school. He knew that if you want to see how strong a church is, find out what their men's ministry is like.

That Wednesday morning seemed at first like it would be the same as usual. It wouldn't. On this particular day, the first sign of my heart coming alive showed up: I said, "Bull Shi#." From there the conversation turned real and raw. I was looking for life answers and I just blurted out what I felt deep down in my heart. I was sick of the religious answers and instructions we were hearing. I wanted to know, "But how, when I leave here, do I apply that to my life? That is a really nice lesson, lots of references to Scripture, but when I leave here, drive out of this parking lot, how do I love my wife better, talk to my son, or hear Jesus talk to me?" Turns out lots of the guys wondered the same thing. They longed as I did from deep in their hearts to know, feel, hear Jesus. Joe Don knew he was in the right place.

Over the next few years, Joe Don became pastor of that small church and we got to know each other well. We found that the lives we lived as boys and young men were similar trails. Our friendship grew.

Since those early days in that Wednesday morning Bible study, we have realized the desperate need for men to get real, heartfelt answers to their questions. We have learned that Jesus does speak to us, guide us, and help us along the way. We have been influenced by incredible men of God. We have fought battles with Satan himself as we learned what brings a man to life in Christ.

Conversations at coffee shops, hunting camps and fire pits, men's groups, bacon and egg breakfasts, and more coffee led to this book.

Both Joe Don and I are committed to the work it takes to live a life where the brokenness of our past does not define who we are today. We have wandered off the trail on many days from past hurts, wounds, and attacks by the evil one, but Jesus is with us. We catch ourselves and recognize Satan's lies sooner. Those things do not define us the way Satan said they did.

When we ask Christ into our hearts, it all changes. You, the guy who does not have Scripture memorized and has on occasion messed up, like yesterday, or this morning. You are not disqualified. Jesus was intentional in choosing men like Joe Don, me, and you. You have the same authority the most famous preacher has in this walk with Jesus. You matter. But that is not enough. We also need something to "ride or die" for. Our families, yes, but something that as a man we can stand back and look at and say, yes, that was a fight worth having—a battle, a rescue mission—and I was part of it. Something that reaches and moves you to the core. You were created for that.

For Joe Don and me, we learned being best friends is hard work. Few men truly have deep close relationships with a best friend. The evil one does not want strong Christian men to be close. It has taken a lot of work for Joe Don and me to learn how to be friends. Adult men wearing our hearts on our sleeves when we need to, learning to stand firm, to call each other out, and to stay alive as a warrior for Jesus in a friendship. Yes, rare in men today. I am not bragging here; hopefully God is talking to your heart. We pray you spend time together with other men cultivating these deep friendships.

Satan wants to create false fronts, the "Poser" John Eldredge calls it. Satan wants men to stay quiet, unengaged, distracted by work, sports, hunting, money, porn. But our hope and prayer for you as you step into this book is to come alive. To step into a life of meaning. To engage in a life that inspires you and the men around you. You are truly important and worthy; the front lines are calling you up. You can call "B.S." when Satan is trying to keep you out of the fight. Calling B.S. may just change your life; it did ours.

   – TJ and Joe Don

INTRODUCTION OF THE STORY
Meet TJ and Joe Don

"Getting to know the men who are going to lead you down a trail is essential. Never ride in a posse when you don't know your lead riders." – TJ Greaney

TJ GREANEY

The little GI home my parents built seemed perfect. A yard with a big climbing tree out back. A boy my age next door to be best friends with. A patch of woods not far one way and the bayou the other. Years later when I went back as an adult, it looked so tiny. The big tree out back was gone. It was hard to understand the feelings I had in my heart that day sitting in my truck out in front. So many memories, so many things that crafted my heart, my mind, my soul.

I was given the gift of being allowed to be a boy in my early years. The sixties in the world's terms were a time of rock and roll, Vietnam protesting, rockets into space, and innovation. I remember my dad worked for an oil company, and occasionally he would sneak my brother and me into the lab and show us dry ice and liquid nitrogen. He built things at our house and took us camping and fishing. We ran barefoot, caught frogs and lizards, snakes and turtles. The trees made for great outlook posts and the ground forts protected us from the enemy. Life was good as far as I knew.

When we moved from the little GI house, I was still young, finishing up the 4th grade. Dad was changing jobs and things were going to be okay. We lived in a rental waiting for a new home to be built in the influential Nassau Bay community just across from NASA, The Manned Spacecraft Center south of Houston. I did not know it at the time, but this was when my eyes to the world around me began to open. Maybe I was just getting older and I was becoming aware of my surroundings. The kids on the blocks around us and my older brother's friends did things I had never thought about. Two boys around the corner from us lived with their mom; their dad had left them. That was the first time I had heard about "divorce."

Kids smoked cigarettes, cussed, stayed out later at night. My eyes were seeing things, my soul was absorbing things, my mind was distracted, and my heart was longing. When I look for my dad around this time, he is not there and memories of Mom begin to fade.

The new house was very prestigious. Our neighbors were astronauts and business leaders, airline pilots and politicians. A bay from the gulf meandered into the entry of the community and there was a lake in the back. I found my way to both quickly. Mom says I used to take a wagon with fishing gear and be gone all day. In those woods, I learned the pain of a bb gun fight and the fear of the darkness. In all that amazing influence, I began learning the effects of drugs and the lure of the female. School became a distant concern. Trouble came in waves, and looking back I ask myself, "Where are Mom and Dad? Why didn't I get in trouble at home for those things?" They never asked me about homework. Sneaking out at night and skipping school had no repercussions at home.

We lost the custom home. Then Mom and Dad rented a two-story white colonial a few blocks over. My innocence and childhood was all but lost. I knew what was happening. I had been moving into a survival mode for years. The answer to everything became drugs and girls. Running on my instincts moved me from one day to the next.

To this day I can remember the smells in the morning at the old white two-story rental house. The rum Dad drank from a coffee cup in the mornings and the stale smell of cigarette smoke blended together. My memories of Dad being around fade quickly. The ones I have around that time are sad and broken. I don't remember Mom there at all. I asked her not long ago where she was at that time. "I was trying to survive. I worked when I could and had to protect your little brother and sisters. I knew I could not do anything for you or your older brother."

Then the day came. Mom left. She packed up everything, my little brother and two little sisters, and left. Dad never came back. The old white house was empty and I was on my own. It was the summer of my 8th grade year. I had just turned 13.

JOE DON FLACK MAYES

I was born Joe Don Flack in Odessa, Texas, in 1950. West Texas is different than the rest of Texas. It's in the desert, and where there is desert there is usually oil. Not for the fainthearted, it's boom or bust in West Texas. Only the tough and resilient survive in this environment.

My given name is Joe Don although my mom and most folks call me "Jody." I am the son of an oil field welder. My dad was tough, hardworking, beer drinking, and loved to fish.

I, like all little boys, looked up to my dad. I looked forward every day to him coming home from work. The smell of his sweat and the oil field was sweet to me. It meant he was home and with me.

On Oct 4, 1952, my dad and I were going to go fishing. Just me and my dad. He would load me in the front seat of his pickup and we would spend the weekend at Robert E Lee Lake where he would teach me to fish.

I awoke early that day and jumped in bed with my dad and mom. Mom told me to "go back to sleep" but the excitement of spending the day fishing with Dad was uncontrollable.

Soon Mom got the bacon and coffee going. Still to this day, those two smells together just feel like home. A place that is safe and filled with the people I love the most.

I daydreamed the ride to the lake, catching fish, and sitting around the campfire listening to my dad's stories. We would snuggle into a sleeping bag and fall asleep counting the stars. The memories would be with me forever.

But at the breakfast table my mom said, "Jody, I just don't feel right about you going with your dad today. I want you to stay with me."

Mom tells the story by describing the tears that flowed from my little eyes. My heart was broken. My dreams were shattered.

The day would now be spent like most other days growing up in West Texas. Playing with my big brother and sister, hunting for horny toads outside, and playing with trucks in the sand. All the time wondering what it would have been like being with my dad. If only Mom would not have said "No."

The news came over the phone: Dad was in a very serious accident in his pickup. A sheep had run out in front of him on the way to the lake. He swerved to miss it and the pickup turned over. He had massive head injuries and was rushed to the hospital. My father died three days later.

Memories of that time forever linger in my mind. Mom crying tears of utter grief and brokenness, lying in her bed with all the lights out, alone. I would enter the room to try and comfort her, but to no avail.

Family members and friends came over. They carried sad faces and food to console her grief. They would hug me in a different way, as if they knew what was ahead for me.

Little did I know, but they were right. I would soon discover the world was not a safe place. As a young boy, I had no idea how much this one episode in my life would affect me.

October 7, 1952, was the worst day of my life. The most important man in my life died. It is really hard to have to say goodbye to someone you love so much. I loved my dad, I needed him, and I missed him. I felt abandoned and all alone.

I would now have to navigate a new path without my dad's love, affection, and example to follow. There were days I would look out the window hoping maybe he would come home from work just one more time. I longed to breathe in the sweet smell of his sweat and the oil field. I would dream of riding next to him in his pickup and going fishing together. It would never happen again. The man I loved the most walked out the door and I never saw him again.

We all have different paths to follow in our lifetimes.

My boyhood path was the hardest of all my years. My mom remarried a man whose wife had died and he had two sons. I now had a step-dad and a new name, Mayes. It is hard for a man to love another man's kids. I experienced it firsthand.

I would grow up searching for the love of my father, but not finding it in the boyhood season of my life. A boy needs a guide on a path when young, but I would have to go it alone.

For most boys, the ages of 1 through 12 are filled with innocence and having fun. For me, there was an emptiness and a feeling of lost-ness and a longing for a past that was gone forever.

Chapter 1
AS A YOUNG BOY:
The Journey Begins
(AGE 0-12)

The heart of a young boy is so good. Scraped knees,
dirty faces, and an innocent smile when he is caught
in the act of being a boy. Thank you Jesus for boys.
But this is also the time in the life of a boy when moments
of joy, sorrow, hurts, and experiences feed the heart,
and markers are left behind.
These markers can shape a man his whole life.

The first 12 years are where a boy begins to show his boyness. He takes risks that Mom goes crazy over but Dad high fives him for. A small hump in the road is a jump for his bike, a tree is made for climbing, a hill is for hiking and sledding down. He loves to explore and can literally get stuck in between a rock and a hard place. He watches his dad with wonder as he uses tools and works in the yard. The boy is a super hero, a range riding cowboy, or a soldier. His toys are the weapons and tools of his male heroes. He still runs to Mom when he gets a cut or a scratch when she is close. When he gets hurt around Dad, he is told to brush it off and continue on, his tears stop and he continues on.

This is where he begins to learn to "do hard things" from Dad. Hugs and "I love you" should flow freely and often from Dad. He is watching Dad closely and will mimic his walk, words, and how he treats his mom. This is where he needs to hear he has what it takes to get things done, make it in this world, and overcome hardships. This is the age he will have the foundations of his faith placed into his heart. He needs to know there is a deeper meaning to life, and that it is Jesus. Youth groups and trips are great at this point. Dad's quest for Jesus can be the example that forms the boy's core understanding of the value and significance of faith in Jesus and walking that out.

Without Dad, the pursuit for authentic manhood and what trail is the right one to ride can be almost impossible. But God loves us, He loves boys and He will offer His guidance. We might not have understood it at the time, but He was there with us. Just like in these stories.

GROWING UP LOST

| TJ |

In 1968 I was 9. It was a simpler time back then, at least for a 9-year-old. No stress from too much television, no internet or video games, just life on life's terms. That year, an amazing film came out that captured my heart and mind, *Oliver*. The movie was a musical story about a group of orphan boys who lived under the guidance of the old man Fagin. Fagin trained them to pick pockets and explained it to them in song. "Pick a pocket or two boys, you have to pick a pocket or two," he sang.

There are a handful of movies that were influential in guiding my heart growing up; *Oliver* was one. *Taxi Driver* another, but that is a story for later. *Oliver* was a tenderhearted orphan boy led astray by a group of street boys when he arrived in the big city alone. Trying to fit in, finding a place, looking to be accepted and loved, everything the street boys had seemed to be what he needed.

In the beginning of the movie, Oliver meets Dodger. Dodger is the leader of the lost boys. He is a bright, street smart, handsome young lad. He sees a chance to bring another boy in, and he knows what Oliver needs to hear. He begins to sing. "Consider yourself at home, consider yourself part of the family. We've taken to you so strong, it's clear we are going to get along." I can see how my heart is drawn to that message, then and now.

My criminal activities as a young man on the streets were almost always done with a hesitant heart. I remember walking the strip center (shopping area) with my best friend during the summers and our goal was to steal something from every shop. We would also follow behind the milkman and steal milk. Most of these antics were boy-level poor choices. I don't think I was looking for attention from my parents or in need of food or other elements of basic survival. We were just bored boys, and that usually leads to trouble. At least it did for us.

As I got older, trying to fill the holes in my heart through acceptance by others often included activities frowned upon by law enforcement. One night a group of guys in a new neighborhood I was living in plotted to break into a liquor store. I went along. When the windows broke, I ran. The two guys who were never afraid went in. I took off behind some houses and into a backyard under a broken down car. This was up north in the winter and there was snow on the ground. Sloppy wet snow. I laid in it for hours, shaking cold as the police walked all around me with flashlights. Hours later, just before sunrise, I slid out and ran home. I remember getting into dry clothes and climbing up into bed. I can feel the emotion of that boy now. I was frightened, confused, worried, but grateful to be in a safe, warm bed. I curled up in a fetal position and fell asleep.

The things I did were never ones that would hurt anybody, not physically. The part that breaks my heart is the boy, the young guy, who didn't have a man there to share with him just how bad the things he was doing could turn out. Most kids inherently know things are not right or good. For most, it is built into us from the very beginning. Of course, there are some human creatures who do not develop the emotional and social elements of their brain that allow them to feel or understand right and wrong. For me, I was taught right and wrong—I just chose wrong.

Criminal activity from our past does not have to define who we are today. Jesus showed us that so clearly as He hung on the cross in those last minutes. The thief cried out and He was there for him. I did a lot of things worse than stealing milk, but today the details don't matter. I made amends where I could, I took my actions to Jesus, and we have dealt with it all.

MATTHEW 6:12–15 And forgive us our debts, as we also have forgiven our debtors. And lead us not into temptation, but deliver us from evil. For if you forgive others their trespasses, your heavenly

Father will also forgive you, but if you do not forgive others their trespasses, neither will your Father forgive your trespasses.

For me, one place I began to find my heart was in a church. My church families have made a huge difference. I found acceptance, kind-hearted direction, meaning. I began to "consider myself at home, consider myself part of the family." As the people of the church, we are to be that place for lost boys, hurting families, tired men.

Dr. Seuss said, "To the world you may be one person, but to one person you may be the world."

If I had written on a piece of paper my biggest dreams in those days on the street, they would have fallen way short of where God has me today. He was my rescue. My heart is tender in this area because I know where a life without Jesus leads. A life lost in this world. Lord, use me to be a voice for You. Lord, use my life today. My challenge to everyone is to find an Oliver in your day, share a smile, a kind word, or maybe even invite them to meet your church family. Invite them home.

YOUR HEART TRAIL

Every little boy wants to be loved and accepted. The role of the father is to provide that for his boy. It is God's design, but what about when the father is absent or disengaged? The little boy still longs for it. So the big question is where does he find it?

Think back into your childhood to who made an impact on your life as a young boy. Who was it that influenced your choices, good or bad? List one or two, with the influence they had. It can be your dad, but for many men, it won't be.

_____

_____

_____

_____

_____

Can you remember a time where you did something you knew ahead of time you should not do? Can you see God prompting you or giving you a nudge to choose differently? Write out the situation and where you think God may have been present with you as a little boy. Good or bad.

_____

_____

_____

_____

_____

Don't be fooled by those who say such things, for bad company corrupts good character. 1 CORINTHIANS 15:33

Come back to your senses as you ought, and stop sinning; for there are some who are ignorant of God—I say this to your shame. 1 CORINTHIANS 15:34

RAISED WITH A TONKA

| TJ |

I was thinking back about Christmas mornings when I was a kid. The fresh cut tree, the colored lights, and the gifts all wrapped. Santa coming and the stories of how close he was and what would happen if we did not get into bed. The idea that Santa was coming was almost overwhelming. So good, so sweet.

Those years, the early years, were very transformative for me. I soaked up everything "boy." I remember walking in the bayous of Houston Texas catching frogs and snakes. We travelled in and out of underground drainage pipes under the city. There was one time my brother had caught a large snapping turtle. He held it to my face and I challenged it, drawing in even closer. Wham, the turtle clamped down on my chin with the force of a bear trap. I was lucky—a few well-placed slaps on its head and I was free. Wounded pretty good but free. We captured some water moccasins one day and called the Houston Zoo to see if they would buy them. I wonder what they were thinking on the other end of the phone when some young boys called them with that question.

I see today how powerful those years were for me. Tree forts, running around the woods, always outside. Always. Christmas was one of the times of the year we would get the gear and the adventure toys we desperately wanted, and some we did not know at the time would inspire us our whole lives.

I remember watching my dad build things. He was good. He built a full-size playhouse, maybe 20' x 20', with a shingled roof. Which I burned down playing with matches. A story for another time. He built a go-cart from an old edger motor and a wagon. He laid a brick patio and built a smoker and flower beds from the same brick. He built a wooden framed cabinet that held cardboard cigar boxes as drawers and each drawer held a surprise. Screws, wire, nuts, and mechanical trinkets that fueled my imagination.

I loved to get screwdrivers and hammers at Christmas. The old saying, "give a boy a hammer and everything looks like a nail," was so true. I don't ever remember getting in trouble for pounding, building, or I am sure destroying something (except the burned down playhouse). The gift of tools was a big deal and said something to my young male heart.

There were a handful of boy toys that became staples. These days they have changed a bit in the materials they are made from but are solids for a young lad. For example, Tonka trucks, cranes, and bulldozers. Big, metal, working toys that fostered hours and hours of digging dirt and rocks at our construction sites. We did not buy jeans with holes in them; we wore holes into them from playing hard. To this day when I see a big piece of machinery working, I am distracted. One of my favorite man toys is an old, rough, well-worn Bobcat tractor I have.

The Red Ryder Daisy BB Gun is of course another. I don't know how much copper we left in the yards around our old house in Houston, but I am sure it would be considered toxic levels today. I won't list the types of varmints and birds that were taken during those years. It was a lot. Boys shoot things when they are training with BB guns, they just do.

My mom tells me stories now of what was going on in those days that I never knew about. My dad was beginning to drink quite a bit. He was unfaithful to their marriage vows. He treated her poorly.

I had no idea. It was years before I suspected anything. The first time it emerged, we were on a family camping trip across America. We had left a National Park and stopped for a night at the Holiday Inn. A huge treat in those days. That night I was awakened by the sound of my mom and dad arguing. Dad had gone out after we all went to sleep and got drunk at a nearby bar. Someone took his wallet and Mom was pissed. I look back now and that was the first time I saw or thought maybe something was not right.

But even so, each year Christmas and birthdays came. The Tonka trucks were unveiled for the construction projects ahead. Our BB supply was refilled and hand tools were distributed. We got telescopes, rocket kits, electronic radio building kits, and Erector sets. Good, hands-on boy training gifts.

I worry about the boys of today who do not get mentored in the way of the tool or outdoors. I saw a commercial recently that had a young man and his male friends calling his mom as he stood next to his car with a flat tire. He had no idea what to do, but luckily he could call his mom for help. What can the wives of tomorrow expect? A husband who can't work a wrench, a circular saw, a screwdriver, or change a flat tire?

Morgan Snyder with Wild at Heart Ministry and *Becoming Good Soil* Podcast talks about how not knowing these skills weighed heavily on his heart. It was something he went to find as an adult man. He was intentional to seek men to train him in all types of areas. Hunters, carpenters, even repairmen hired to fix things at his home or on his cars became mentors. He pushed into the lessons they taught. The builder, fixer, and provider. Growing as a man of confidence and strength.

Snyder says, "Almost every culture predating the modern world had a process of initiating boys into men. In some cultures, male initiation was intentional, deeply ritualized, and publicly celebrated. In other cultures, male initiation precipitated indirectly but with equal effectiveness because the survival of the culture depended upon it." Snyder references the book *Iron John* by Robert Bly reminding us, "The traditional ways of raising sons, which lasted for thousands and thousands of years, amounted to fathers and sons living in close—murderously close—proximity, while the father taught the son a trade; perhaps farming or carpentry or black-smithing or tailoring..."

Time for boys to experience life with men is essential. Christmas toys for boys can be a catalyst for their hearts, but it must be paired with training. Buy a birdhouse to build, but build it with them. A bow and arrow or BB gun requires training. Cultivating a boy's heart with toy trucks and tractors can be lifelong investments in their confidence levels and ability to care for their family. So important.

With all the brokenness and heartaches my mom endured, with all the battles with the evil forces that taunted my father most of his life, still they blessed me in a huge way. They let me be a boy. To this day, I love to build things and have trained my boys with hammers and nails, saws and wrenches. I have a set of drawers in my garage full of screws and nails and wire nuts. We love the outdoors, hunting, fishing, adventure, and a good campfire.

Gift giving to boys can be a powerful time if it is thought out. It may not be what they want, but what they need. Even in the brokenness of my home, God was working. God uses everything for His good.

♥ YOUR HEART TRAIL ♥

A boy is easily influenced by things. His inherent design is a critical building block for who he is and how he handles himself as he grows. Even the smallest things create lifelong markers in their lives. Hands-on lessons are the most impressive teaching tools for a boy. A boy learns from the things his hands do.

What crafts or skills did you learn as a boy? Something that took your hands. Who taught you? Example: A wooden birdhouse, a go-cart, Lego building with your uncle.

_____

_____

_____

_____

Did your dad or another close male role model have the ability to teach you something but did not, and your heart longed for it? Who was it and what was it? Example: I wish my grandfather would have taught me to raise tomatoes. He was a master at it. I wish my dad would have taught me to fix cars. He was always working on cars. My grandpa built our deck by hand, but I was too little to help. I wish I had been older.

_____

_____

_____

_____

_____

May the favor of the Lord our God rest on us; establish the work of our hands for us—yes, establish the work of our hands. PSALM 90:17

The hardworking farmer should be the first to receive a share of the crops. 2 TIMOTHY 2:6

CHAPTER 1
BIBLE STUDY

OPENING DISCUSSION
QUESTIONS *15 minutes*

Go around the circle and have the men answer one of the questions.

➡ Which one of the Heart Trails spoke to you? Why?

➡ How would you describe the Young Boy Stage of your life?

LEADER: How many of you men had a dad that was a strong spiritual leader in your home growing up? (Raise your hands.)

If you were able to raise your hand, then take a moment and thank God, for you are a blessed man. Most men did not have a healthy father who loved God with all his heart, and his family with the same passion. The goal is to *"return the heart of the father to his sons and daughters."* Our hope is after you complete this study you will be on the path to becoming more of the man God wants you to be.

For the next few weeks you will see that even the greatest of God's men go through very hard times and are flawed. God can use us in spite of our weaknesses or past mistakes.

BIBLE STUDY
25 minutes

Take turns reading out loud.

Moses as a Boy

Moses was a great man of God, but suffered extreme hardships throughout most of his life in preparation to lead God's people at the age of 80. If you feel like you have not been used by God yet, then be encouraged.

Unless you are over 80, you have no excuses, and even if you are, there is still more to come.

Moses had many weaknesses and flaws, including a speech problem (stuttering), and was a very reluctant leader. He was insecure, scared, and felt inadequate to be used by God. If that sounds like you, then you are in good company with Moses.

In today's lesson we are going to look at Moses' life as a boy. If you had a really hard first 13 years of your life, you will identify with Moses. If you grew up in a blessed home, stay with us; God will reveal to you why you are here. His Word and your commitment will not come back empty.

The Birth of Moses

Read Exodus 2:1–10

LEADER: Put yourself in Moses' family's shoes. What would you have done in the circumstances they were in? Would you have the faith to trust God and send your baby down a crocodile-infested river? (Discuss God's supernatural protection and provision for Moses in his Young Boy stage of life.)

> "Moses' [boyhood years] were difficult, lonely years. He must have wept night after night in the privacy of his palace room, his tears soaking into the royal linen sheets. No soothing touch from his mother. No comforting words from his father. No smile from his sister Miriam, or playful antics from his brother Aaron. It is easy to imagine the young lad pouring out his heart to the God he had learned to seek." – Chuck Swindoll, *Moses*

LEADER: Bullet Points

➡ Before Moses was even born, he had a death sentence pronounced on him by the King of the land.

➡ God protected Moses' life, but he was separated from his family after being weaned.

➡ Moses' boyhood was really hard.

➡ Even God's chosen men are not exempt from hard times.

APPLICATION
10 minutes

LEADER: There are no accidents with God. *"All things work together for good to those who are called according to His purpose,"* Scripture says. Moses overcame all his hardship as a young boy. He learned and prospered in Pharaoh's home, but made a big mistake when he was 40 and killed a man. It would be 40 years before he was finally ready to be used by God at the age of 80.

Perhaps you suffered the crushing fracture of your home by the divorce of your parents or loss of a parent. Maybe you moved from one home to another, and the memories of loneliness linger. Maybe you spent time in a foster home living with total strangers. Most men have experienced hardship during at least one season of their lives.

You may not have a hardship memory and your thoughts are of good and happy times. Stay with us here.

We see in the life of Moses that hard times build character and prepare us to be better men, dependent on God our Father. That can be a very churchy statement. We know—and it can be brutal to piece that lesson together with what we have suffered. The word "Father" when our dad walked out on us? The hurts we carry, the things we see in the world happening to our kids or others. Child abuse, human trafficking, electronic media pounding our kids every day. We read the Word and know it as truth, but to access our hearts with acceptance, forgiveness, and solutions can be difficult.

So what is God preparing you for? What has He already prepared you for? There is something up ahead He needs you to take care of for Him. Moses used all the excuses, so don't waste your time trying to get out of it. The hurts and brokenness, the blessings and joyfulness are yours. They are personal and you have walked in them. That is where He starts. Your personal testimony is where you have been perfectly trained.

CLOSING CONVERSATION

What was the most difficult thing you went through as a boy? Did you see God then? Do you see God in it now? Example: My dad worked all the time; I am not going to do that to my kids.

_____

_____

_____

_____

_____

_____

_____

_____

_____

ACTION STEP

➡ If you had a great boyhood and suffered no trauma, then thank God and either call or write your parents (parent/step-parent/grandparent) and thank them for the protection they provided.

➡ If you were like TJ and Joe Don, with hard boyhoods, thank God for seeing you through. Write out at least one lesson you learned that God had His hand on.

➡ Should you step into mentoring a boy who might not have a man in his life today?

➡ Forgive or begin to forgive your dad and mom for any hurts they caused or allowed. Write out the hurts and your thoughts.

✝ CLOSING PRAYER

Thank You Father for the gift of life. You were the one who created me in my mother's womb, and You gave me life. I want to learn to honor both my dad and mom and to appreciate what love and provision they may have provided for me. Help me to forgive them when they were not there. I thank You for the tough times Lord and how You will craft them to make me a better man. Use me Lord as a man for You in my world. Help me to hear You speak as I seek You. I love You Lord. Amen.

Chapter 2

THE TEENAGE BOY AND HIS JOURNEY

(AGE 13-18)

The awkward school dance, confused about girls, and pushing the limits with Mom and Dad. Whether you loved them or hated them, the teen years are hard for almost every boy. Words from peers and a desire to be a part of a group can take control here. My nose is too big, my ears stick out, my legs are so skinny. "Hey, try this; come on, everyone is doing it." Boys start to become aware of their bodies and things begin to change. They grow hair in places not seen before. Testosterone begins to percolate and cause certain parts of their body to do things. Their mind gets a bit scrambled and crazy. They desperately want answers but don't ask or have anyone to ask. They need to know what is going on but many times get bad information from other teens or the Internet.

Today electronics can wreck a teen boy's heart and dreams. Being strung out on video games can cause laziness and a lack of desire to move their bodies. Their worth is defined by likes on social media posts.

A teen boy will begin to disengage with his mom and push back now. He should be defining his masculinity. Who and what a guy is. Without a healthy male role model, he may be adrift. Some may be so confused about boyhood and teen maleness that they seek all sorts of sexual identities. They deeply desire and long for the validation of their father or other men in their lives.

WANDERING ABOUT

| TJ |

I left school on the first day of 9th grade and wandered around the neighborhood a few weeks. With everyone in school, there was really nothing for me. I decided to hitchhike to California and find a friend who moved there with her mom. I made it there but to a less than open invite. I quickly hitched north to the Arrowhead Lake area to see my close friend Evans. During our junior high years, we were inseparable. His family moved about the same time mine split. His parents loved me and allowed me to stay a while. Drugs quickly became a cornerstone of my daily activities. I realized there was going to be nothing there for me. Even if there could have been, I did not understand what to do.

I longed for family and decided to hitch to Illinois to see my mom, brother, and sisters. The trail from California to Illinois went through Las Vegas where I was arrested for sleeping on the side of an Interstate on-ramp. Being a juvenile, I was kept until Mom could be contacted. I remember them walking me onto the plane a few days later, sitting me down with a firm warning, "Don't come back."

I had dreams of a good life in small town Illinois. There was really nothing bad about it; I could have done well there. Mom enrolled me in school, but that didn't last. Again, I turned to girls, drugs, and crime to answer the questions I had. Does anyone care about me? Can I mean something to someone? When I had drugs or challenged authority, I got attention. I lied, cheated, and stole even from my grandmother.

Mom did the best she could. She pleaded, had people come over and talk to me, put me in juvenile jail for a weekend to try and get my attention. Nothing. Then there was the mental hospital.

When they placed me in the state hospital, I knew I had to get out of Illinois. I crafted an escape and took off. I was hiding out from the police in a drug house when I blacked out from an overdose. I woke up and had no idea what day it was or how long I was out. It was morning. I made my way to my grandmother's. I blew in the back door and down into the basement. I gathered a few things, including the shotgun my dad had given me two years earlier on my birthday. Mom was standing to the side of the back door and asked me what I was doing as I ran up the stairs and out the door. I don't remember answering. She watched me run down the street, shotgun in hand. She told me later that she knew at that point there was nothing else she could do for me but pray.

I traded that gun for drugs and hopped a freight train headed south. I made it back to Houston. All the drugs I had traded for, I used. I found myself again lost, alone, and confused on the streets.

As I wandered about, I met Danny. We became fast friends. Danny's parents found out I had no place to live and they offered me a room in their small home. It was a no-brainer for me but a poor decision for them. I was a terrible influence on Danny.

The one rule I was told I had to follow was that church was on Sunday and I had to go. Their church was a lot different than the Catholic ones I knew as a young boy. It was a small Bible church, whatever that was. What I found was that they actually read the Bible, talked about it, did life together as a church family. During that time, I was mentored by a man named Terry. He shared Christ with me, and I eventually gave my life to Jesus and was baptized. It was not an outward life transformational thing for me. I still kept doing all the things I was doing; I just did them after church. I eventually left my friend's house and moved out on my own. But that day, the one where I asked Jesus into my heart, I believe that day the Holy Spirit began to work on me deep inside.

I found work on construction sites as a carpenter's helper. It was a boot camp experience in the Texas sun for a young man. I learned to work hard. I did not know it at the time, but I desperately wanted those men to like me and accept me into their group. I found their approval when I showed up on time, moved fast, and kept things organized on the job site.

I lived a double life. I was a great employee, worked hard, and kept myself in line on the job. I was a good young man in my heart and people liked me. But then there was the dark side where drugs, breaking the law, and making poor choices always seemed to rise up and cost me the good I had worked for.

I lived through head-on collisions, drug use, and my apartment windows being shot out from a drug deal gone bad. Slowly my heart and my body were becoming weary. I was jealous of my friends. Why do they get to live in a home with both parents and I don't? Why did I get this life? What do I have to do to get out of this, or is this the best it will ever get? I think back now and it makes me sad for that young man.

GOING IT ALONE ON THE WRONG PATH

| JOE DON |

In a time of life when days should be filled with playing and adventure, there always seemed to be a dark cloud over my head. Why doesn't my step-dad love me? What have I done? What can I do to get him to love me?

"The deepest wound a man carries is his father wound."
– John Eldredge

I discovered early in life the world is not a safe place.

Our house was small but our outdoors was big in Midland, Texas. We played outside all the time and my memories are full of catching horny toads, football in the street, baseball in the vacant lot, and hide and go seek at night.

My best friends were my four brothers and two sisters. We were together all the time. I think we gave each other the assurance that we were okay and normal. Deep down we knew we weren't. Our family was dysfunctional and filled with fighting and turmoil. We never had enough money and the pressure to just survive was overwhelming at times to us all. Both my parents drank to self-medicate their life pain. They fought every night, yelling mean words and throwing dishes at one another. My home was not a safe place to be.

My earliest prayers were cries for help: "God if you are there, would you please make my parents quit fighting?" Nights were long, tears soaked my pillow, and my prayers went unanswered.

But kids are resilient and we all survived, but not without wounds.

I loved sports. I played every sport I could and it became my identity. I loved the competition and became known as a player who would "run through a wall" for a coach. Looking back now, I know I was motivated by my need for approval from a man.

"A young man's heart is wounded when he has no one to take him into the adventures his soul craves, no one to show him how to shoot a free throw or jump his bike or rock climb or use a power tool. This is how most young men experience fatherlessness - there is no man around who cares and who is strong enough to lead him into anything." - John Eldredge, Fathered by God

A broken leg heals much faster than a broken heart. I know that firsthand. I so wanted my stepdad to come to one of my games. Just one time to show me he cared. It never happened.

My mom was overprotective and I was made fearful by her attempts to keep me from getting hurt. Adventure was something to avoid because of what happened to my dad. She loved me but in unhealthy ways.

This season of my life was consumed with sports and hard work. Playing sports was the passion of my life. Every moment was consumed with either playing, practicing, or reading about and watching sports.

My goal was to one day play professional basketball with the Boston Celtics. First, I had to get a scholarship so I could go to college. I remember the day when I realized my dreams would never be realized. I wept.

"Sons need fathers who are involved in their lives—dads who will love them, teach them, and discipline them. But clearly, sons also need a masculine vision. They need a manhood language." - Robert Lewis, Modern-Day Knight

I poured myself into hard work. I worked after school busting tires at the tire store so I could pay for my gas and insurance on my 1957 Chevy. I cruised the streets of Midland drinking beer with my buddies and chasing girls. I was forced into independence and had to pay for everything I needed. I had no safety net or even an allowance from my parents. In order to survive, I had to work and do it with great effort. No one was there to rescue me if I failed.

The summer of my senior year in high school I worked for my granddad in Odessa. He, like my real dad, was a hard, tough oil field worker. I discovered firsthand what my life would have been if my dad had not been killed.

I have never worked so hard in all my life. We woke at 4 am to drive to the job. Arrive at sunrise and work till dark outside in the West Texas heat. Drive home to eat dinner at 8 pm, and go to bed to do it all over again the next day.

One early morning in the pickup going to the job, I was sitting between my granddad and one of his workers. He introduced me, "Charlie, you know whose boy this is (referring to me)?" My granddad said, "This is Don Flack's boy."

There was a pause and then the man said, "Son, your dad was the hardest working man in this oil field, and everyone loved your dad." It had been 15 years since my dad died and it was the first time I had heard words of affirmation about my dad. I felt so proud to be the son of Don Flack. I still missed him greatly.

I knew the oil field was not for me. That fall and for the next two years I went to college, worked at the YMCA, and searched for my meaning and purpose. I ended up quitting college. I took all the wrong paths in life for the next three years. I hit the bottom in 1973. Alcohol, drugs, and rock and roll had taken its toll.

I needed guidance, direction, a man to follow and help lead me into the path of real manhood. I felt all alone, isolated, and wounded.

More Stories Along the Young Man's Journey

A "NEW NAME"
| TJ |

I was born into a Catholic family in 1959. From what I can tell, it was a pretty standard family of that day. Five kids, mom stayed home, and dad worked. I was the second of the five — three boys, two girls. Brother, me, sister, brother, sister. We, for the most part, carry the traditional Catholic names of our forefathers, grandmothers, and saints.

I am Thomas Joseph. My grandfather and great-grandfather had the same name. The family history is a checkered past with stories of troubled lives and mysterious happenings. Some of the stories have never been confirmed and probably won't be. I used to think they were cool, now not so much.

Recently, I thought about my name and the apostle Thomas. Thomas was one of Jesus' 12. He was lesser known and, like many of the others, had a different name, Didymus, before Jesus came along. Jesus liked to change their names.

I grew up as Tom. Mom and Dad called me Tom Tom when I was good and Thomas Joseph when I wasn't. I heard the latter one frequently as I got older.

Names back in the old country were many times given to a person to describe who they were or would become. Bob Carpenter was a woodworker; John Smith, a blacksmith; Betty Crocker, a cook. Names in the new world did not always follow that trend; they created tough names like Buck, Wyatt, Jessie, and Hop-a-Long.

I believe that kids can take on their names, become a namesake. Say a Doubting Thomas might be a guy who is always in trouble or a bit of a misbehaver but has a great heart and the sweetest disposition. He can be a bit of a skeptic and learn a lot of things the hard way. He is probably really handsome and had great hair as a teen.

We speak into our children about who they are at a young age. If you tell them they are bad, stupid, or are never going to amount to anything, guess what — you're speaking it over them. If parents, the most important people in the world to them, tell them they are not worthy of great things, it can be devastating. A boy can carry for his whole life the time his father called him an idiot.

Thank God we have a loving Father who does not care about any of those things that you may have been told as a child. Thank goodness He loves us no matter what and teaches us how to forgive.

"And when you stand praying, if you hold anything against anyone, forgive him, so that your Father in heaven may forgive you your sins." Mark 11:25

❤ YOUR HEART TRAIL ❤

Do you like your name? Are you named after a favorite grandfather or uncle? Do you know why your parents gave you that name? Write out some thoughts on your name.

Do you have a nickname? Does it have good connotations behind it or does it remind you of painful times? Make notes here.

Note: Do not accept a nickname that comes from brokenness and the lips of the evil one. If you are a Christ follower, your "new" name is Beloved Son of God.

He who has an ear, let him hear what the Spirit says to the churches. To him who overcomes, to him I will give some of the hidden manna, and I will give him a white stone, and a new name written on the stone which no one knows but he who receives it. Revelation 2:17

To them I will give in My house and within My walls a memorial, and a name better than that of sons and daughters; I will give them an everlasting name which will not be cut off. Isaiah 56:5

TAXI DRIVER

| TJ |

I left the theatre wandering around the neighborhood nearby. I was transfixed on the characters from the movie. I was also in love. Not with a cute, young girl from my high school class, but the young girl in the movie. I was 17 and had emotions I did not understand and no one to talk to about them.

Looking back, beginning in my early teens I was enamored with girls. I have a journal from back then, and one thing I have noticed was that every chapter describes a fixation on a different girl. It was not about sex. It was about acceptance, care, loneliness. I was in love. I was betrayed. I was jealous. I was confused. My emotions were all over the map. My hormones were raging and my brain undeveloped.

My mom and dad split when I was 13. The few times I did get to circle back around and see my dad, I had no idea what to say or ask about becoming a man. I didn't know how to talk about girls, work, faith, or life. He never offered anything on his own. I don't remember one time that he asked, "How are you son?"

A boy will have questions that need specific answers, and without them he will trail blaze by emotion. If it feels good, go that way. If it is scary, go over there. Bail out if it gets hard, run if you have to. Do the best you can or check out. Drugs, sex, and alcohol masked the insecure and terrifying. Oh, if I got a reaction from someone, then that is what I would do or say or be. I was starved for attention, meaning, acceptance.

Today video games and the internet become the place those questions get answered for many boys, and men who are still seeking the answers. Likes on a social media page or viewing pornographic content become an addiction. Depression and anxiety swell to a fevered pitch. And, sorry ladies, not even the most loving mother or prestigious female therapist can repair this gaping wound.

A friend recently called and told me about a fatherless boy who was being bullied. His mom had pulled him out of school. It made me think of when I was in junior high. I was bullied by the classic two-guy team. I didn't have the option to get out. I had to deal with it. I wonder what that boy's father would have said to him. Would he have taught him a left hook or a round-house kick? I wonder how boys today will learn to fight through hard times if they are not taught. Moms and others may cringe at this comment. What if something happens to you or your daughter? I suspect you would want your husband, her husband or boyfriend to stand up, step in, and fight to protect you, her, your family. Boys need to learn to fight evil.

Every job, every trade, comes with training. You get a job as a fry cook helper, you learn to flip burgers and fry fries from the cook. Whether you cut lawns or insert cardiovascular stints—you have to be trained. I don't think I want my doctor to be untrained when he begins to cut me open. For that matter, I don't want the electrician, plumber, or tree guy to work on my house if he has not been trained in the skills he is offering. No way. Since the beginning of time, the boy has been trained in the way of manhood by his father and the men around him.

When it comes to training a boy to understand why he is feeling the way he is, why his body does that, and how to react to those feelings, our world is falling short. The most notable reason today is that, again, there is no man in the house to teach them the way of a man. Sadly, many times today's adult man did not have a good role model either and lacks the skills to teach the boy even if he is in the house. Fear sets in and what information that is translated is communicated in an unhealthy way. There are also the locker room lessons. "Boy, just make sure if you drink, don't overdo it." "Make sure you use a condom, son." "That's my boy—the girls love him," yuk, yuk, fist bump. This is all crap, and the men who lead their boys this way are fear-packed meatheads.

The movie I watched that night was *Taxi Driver*. I re-watched parts of it recently and thought, "Oh my goodness, I would not want my boys watching this." I was embarrassed by the vocabulary alone. That night as a lost teen boy, after the movie I wandered around the neighborhood crying out "I love you" for the young prostitute portrayed in the movie by Jody Foster. It was not the idea of having sex with her; it was to rescue her. I was a street kid and she was a street kid. She was being taken advantage of and I wanted to save her, care for her, give her what I didn't have. It was a movie but it moved me. My wounded and confused boy heart just could not process it. It was so deep inside. I was so lost in how to handle any of the things I was feeling. Today, looking back, it was really me crying out for myself.

Good men fight to overcome the hardships they bring to marriage and fatherhood. No man will get this exactly right. But a man who has committed his life to Jesus has a chance, no matter his past. The Navy Seals have a saying, "All in, All the time." A boy needs to learn that early to become a warrior for his family, his church, his friends, and most of all, Jesus.

❤ YOUR HEART TRAIL ❤

Have you ever had a movie move you? Name one and how it affected you. (It does not have to be bad or when you were a boy.)

_____

_____

_____

_____

Who was your mentor or guide when you were a teen or in your early twenties who helped you navigate a hard situation? Example: A coach helped me when I lost my dad. He was always encouraging. A boss I had really helped me learn to be a carpenter even when I messed up all the time. My dad was always there; he talked to me about (what topics and conversations).

_____

_____

_____

_____

When I was a child, I used to speak like a child, think like a child, reason like a child; when I became a man, I did away with childish things.
1 Corinthians 13:11

CHAPTER 2
BIBLE STUDY

OPENING DISCUSSION
QUESTIONS *15 minutes*

Go around the circle and have the men answer one of the questions.

➥ What was one of the Heart Trails that spoke to you?

➥ How would you describe the Teenage Journey (13-18) of your life?

LEADER: The teenage years are some of the most difficult for young men. Biologically their bodies are changing from boys to men, but so are the expectations placed upon them. There is a yearning for real adventure and a need to be assured he "has what it takes to be a real man." As a young man it is a time to learn by doing instead of by being told. A boy without an active father or mentor will make many mistakes along the way.

He discovers life is hard and filled with extreme challenges. He must learn to get up after he has been knocked down.

BIBLE STUDY
25 minutes

Take turns reading out loud.

Two basic reasons God has given us the Old Testament is to study first for instruction and secondly for hope. Joseph had an incredibly difficult cowboy season, and yet got himself up and made something great of his life.

Joseph in the Teenage Years

Read Genesis 37:1-4

Jacob was an old man when Joseph was born. Joseph was his dad's favorite. Joseph had ten half-brothers, one full brother, and one half-sister.

Jacob was a tired and rather passive father. He was not very involved in the lives of his children. He is a classic illustration of a man too busy, tired, and uninvolved in his role as a father.

At the age of 17, Joseph had dreams from God that made his brothers angry.

Read Genesis 37:5-11

Joseph's brothers plotted to kill their brother out of jealousy.

Read Genesis 37:17-20

Jealousy drove the brothers to put him in a cistern and sell him to a caravan carrying perfume and spices to Egypt. The brothers put goat's blood on Joseph's colorful coat given to him by his father and told their dad Joseph was dead.

Joseph had to grow up too soon at the age of 17. He was separated from his family, but watch how God uses his hardship to grow him into a man of God.

After arriving in Egypt, Joseph was sold to Potiphar, the Captain of Pharaoh's Guard. Potiphar saw that Joseph had God's favor and put him in charge of his household, then of all he owned. The only thing Potiphar worried about was the food he ate.

Joseph lost it all when he was falsely accused of rape by Potiphar's wife and was thrown in prison. But God was with him.

After being released from prison, he rose to the position of Pharaoh's right-hand man after interpreting Pharaoh's dreams.

In the last days of Jacob's life (Joseph's dad), he and all of his sons were starving due to a famine. They went to Pharaoh to appeal for food and, lo and behold, Joseph was the man in position to make the decision that saved his family.

So Joseph assigned the best land of Egypt, the region of Rameses, to his father and his brothers, and he settled them there, just as Pharaoh had commanded. And Joseph provided food for his father and his brothers in amounts appropriate to the number of their dependents, including the smallest children. Genesis 47:11–12

LESSONS TO LEARN:

➡ Joseph was favored by his father over his other brothers and sister, and they knew it and it bothered them greatly.

➡ Joseph's brothers turned against him.

➡ Even when Joseph was trying his best to do what was right, things went wrong. He was accused of rape even when he did the right thing and ran.

➡ Joseph forgave his brothers. After all he went through, he blessed them in the end.

 **APPLICATION**
10 minutes

LEADER: Most of us can remember brokenness in our families. There were situations we were forced to deal with that at the time seemed insurmountable. Imagine the feelings and thoughts Joseph had when he was cast into the pit and left to die by his own brothers. Ours may not have been so dramatic. Maybe we just felt like we could not connect with our brothers or sisters, maybe we had step-brothers or -sisters and never felt a part of. Maybe you had a great family growing up but had a friend who you knew was lost.

When Joseph ran from Potiphar's wife, the right thing to do, he was accused and suffered hardship. How can God allow things like that to happen?

One thing consistent in Joseph's life was that he believed and listened for God to speak to him. He trusted Him. It almost seems it would be impossible with all that happened to him to stay in a close relationship with God. But he did. The fruit that came from trusting and listening, following God even through his hardships, paid off. In the moment it may be, will be, hard to do. But the examples God gives us over and over are that He is with us and He will prevail.

Every man needs other men. You need men close to you, ones who know your story. When those life difficulties come crashing down around you, you find yourself in a pit, accused, facing hardships, you need other men there. These other men need to be trusted with reminding you to stay with God; they need to be men of prayer and honor. They must hold you accountable and responsible. They love you despite your past and because they know what God will do with you in the future. You need them and they need you.

CLOSING CONVERSATION

What hardship in life has knocked you down and was there a lesson you learned? Share it with the others as an encouragement.

_____

_____

_____

_____

If you are facing a hardship, share it now so others can carry the yoke with you. You do not have to ride this trail alone.

ACTION STEPS

➥ Take time this week and meet one-on-one with one of the men in your group. You don't have to do a Bible study together. Eat some BBQ, go fishing, watch a game, drink coffee. Just begin a relationship.

➥ Don't call these men "accountability partners." These men are becoming your friends, and this is what friends do. They watch out for each other, hold each other responsible to make good choices. They ride, fight, do life together.

➥ Write out a true teenage boy story that was good. One where you and a buddy or some buddies went on an adventure. Be reminded of the great fish caught, the campfires at night, the things you saw. Be reminded of the laughter and the adrenaline, the fear and the accomplishments.

 **CLOSING PRAYER**

My Father in Heaven, I want to thank you for the tough times in my life. I now know they were not meant to defeat me, but instead to mold me into a more Godly man. I want to learn what You are teaching me so that I can be a mighty man of God and I can be used of You to bring hope to others through my life story. In Jesus' name.

Chapter 3

THE YOUNG MAN TRAIL

(20s)

Direct your children
onto the right path,
and when they are older,
they will not leave it.
– Proverbs 22:6

A teen grows into a young man in his twenties. This is a time where he looks for answers and begins to explore his own trail. His testosterone is flowing. He will explore the whole thing about girls and sex if he has not already. Heartbreak and mood swings happen. He will take bigger risks. His desire to be a part of a group, to be known, is important to him. He begins to look for meaning, but rarely knows what it could be. He desperately needs to have good men around him. Society and Satan will be working hard to take him out.

Many young men do not launch into manhood well. Continued training is important with finances, relationships, and tools. This is a time for tough love and lots of prayer from parents. It may be the most taxing prayer time for parents. The young man needs to step into the role of providing for himself, into being a man. He should have a foundation built on Christ, but may struggle traveling that trail. He may wander from his faith, and he needs a consistent example by his parents and mentors, which assures him that Jesus is real when he is ready to circle back.

EXCEEDING MY PLAN

| TJ |

I met my first wife in my early twenties. The courtship was based on a lot of the survival character traits I lived by. Lodging, food, and acceptance were all core needs for me. Her mom ran an apartment complex and offered us a free apartment after we found out she was pregnant. She worked in the office and I began doing maintenance work there.

The relationship was on and off, but one thing I felt deep inside, we had to get married. I could not let our baby be without a dad on the birth certificate. During one of our on-again periods, we were married by a Justice of the Peace. Our son was born and I was there.

I had no idea how to be a father or a husband. Everything I did was out of instinct and survival from some place deep inside I did not understand. I had a desire to care for my son; I had a desire to do better in life. I think I was a good guy. I was fair, learned how to work hard. I also know now that my mother-in-law wanted to try and keep me around. She knew my son needed a dad. She made it possible in a tough situation.

I was sitting on the couch one Saturday morning smoking pot. Cartoons were on the television and my son walked up to me and asked me a question. I realized as he turned to walk away that I had ignored him. He asked a question and I just stared into the television. God spoke to me as he walked away, "You just missed your son talking to you. His first questions and you missed it." It was almost audible. I have never forgotten that moment. I know now it was God.

After a run on some pretty heavy drugs not long after that, I heard that voice again. It was not as loud, but I could feel it. I knew I could not live the way I was living much longer. My wife had moved out, my son was going to be affected. I would lose everything. My older brother had been calling me and asking if I had had enough. He was sober in AA and he said I did not have to keep doing what I was doing. Everything I knew was crashing down on me and I was desperate for relief. I went to my first 12-step meeting. I met people who had lived the same stories I had. They had been to the bottom and walked in the darkness I was experiencing. They shared how they had managed to piece together some time without drugs. Things were going well for them. I wanted that. I felt a lot of relief, fear, and excitement that night. I walked up front at the end of the meeting and confessed I was an addict and wanted to change my life.

Our little family was short-lived, but my commitment to my son and then my sobriety was never a question for me. I stayed close in proximity to his mom. I would take him any time I could. I would forgo any other plans. I began to be serious about a job. Working, earning a living, taking care of my son's needs. In a lot of ways, it was good. I was clean and sober and active in the 12-step program and events. My son and I did a lot of fishing back in those days. Anytime we could go, we went, and we built a catalog of memories from the adventures.

My ex-mother-in-law was amazing. She promoted our time together and offered me all types of small repair projects. I eventually began a small construction company doing the same repairs I did for her with other apartment managers in the area. The business grew. I remember saving up and buying an old pickup truck for work. I learned how to keep my books and other requirements from a retired executive at SCORE (Service Corps of Retired Executives). I soaked up the lessons and hungered for the guidance by Mr. Adams, my counselor. He taught me to keep my books with a pencil and paper, scolded me if I spent frivolously, and was patient to a fault. To this day, I refer to lessons he taught me. I longed for the counsel of a seasoned mentor and a loving older man. He offered it freely.

I hired and paid for private counseling for several years. There were breakthroughs in a lot of areas. When it came to girls, dating, and all that crazy stuff, I knew I was messed up. I took a year sabbatical from dating just to clear my head. One rule I kept was that if I had my son, I would limit his exposure to the women I was dating. For the most part, I worked when I did not have him, participated in my 12-step meetings, and when I did have him, we fished.

When he was 8, I met Sandra. She was an apartment manager and asked me to come look at some work at her complex. I was not looking for a relationship and in a lot of ways we were exact opposites. She was a young, pretty blond and busy with her friends, career, and all the things a young, pretty, single girl does. Eventually we did begin dating. I loved her joyful spirit and she was beautiful. She apparently liked my bum (rear end) and that I was a good single dad, did not party, and was focused on building a business.

Not long before we met, I had purchased my first house. It was a serious fixer-upper, but being in the business, I dove in and remodeled it to fit the styles of the day. She tells the story of the first time I invited her over for dinner and she pulled up in the driveway. As she looked around, she told herself, "I could live here." Little did I know; little did she know. We were married a year later.

Sandra had a deep desire to be a part of a church. We found a home church and dove in with both feet. Service work, volunteering, training classes, and Bible studies all became an intricate part of our lives. We both longed for family, and older, wiser adults in our lives. We found it in our church and thrived.

I can see now how God walked me through so many pieces of my life story. The desperate moments were the platforms He would build on later. If I had written on a piece of paper back in my early twenties the best life I could ever have dreamed of, I would have come up way short of where He was taking me and His plans for what was to come.

DISCOVERING THE RIGHT PATH

| JOE DON |

Realizing I was lost and hopeless I wanted to run, but where would I run? I ran to Denver where my sister lived. Just after I arrived, she set me up on a blind date with a girl she worked with.

We were going pick her up after her softball game. When we arrived, we found three girls' softball games going. Sitting on a hill overlooking the fields, my sister asked me, "See if you can pick her out." I of course replied, "I have never seen her before." Her sisterly reply, "Just see if you can pick her out."

So I began to check out three fields full of beautiful, young, athletic women, which wasn't a painful exercise for a young heathen womanizer like me. Finally, I arrived at my conclusion, "I hope it is that center-

fielder on the middle field." Astounded, my sister replied, "That is her."
I felt like I had just won the lottery. Little did I know, I won far beyond
any million-dollar lottery that day.

I fell in love at first sight. She was the most beautiful woman I had
ever seen in my life. We had a great time on our date. When I was
taking her home she asked, "Would you like to go to church with me
tomorrow?" It caught me by complete surprise. I had been to church
less than ten times in my entire life, and church was the last thing on
my mind at that moment. Of course I agreed—I would have gone to a
Beethoven symphony with this chick. Considering I had just seen the
Rolling Stones in concert, Beethoven would have been the supreme
sacrifice.

We went together to a little Baptist church on Sunday night and
I heard the Gospel of Jesus preached by a fiery young preacher from
Baylor University who literally scared the hell out of me, almost. I
grabbed her hand and said, "We need to get out of here." I breathed a
breath of relief when we left without anyone seeing us, or so I thought.

The next day I took her to work in downtown Denver and got pulled
over by a cop, a big cop. After informing me of my violation of the law
he said, "You look familiar." I quickly informed him that could not be. I
was from Texas and just got in town two days before. I was thinking to
myself, "Do I have any pot in the car?"

He then asked me a question that floored me, "Were you by chance
in a little Baptist church last night?" Busted, "Yes sir I was." To which he
replied, "If you come back next Sunday, I will not write you a ticket." I
had absolutely no idea what grace was, but I had just gotten a heavy dose
of it.

I arrived at the church the next Sunday and he was waiting on the
front porch for me to arrive. I got out of the car with my long hair, bell
bottom jeans, and t-shirt, and walked up to the Big Cop. He hugged me
and said, "I love you man."

What? I had never been hugged by a man or told by a man I was
loved. Who was this man? What made him want to do that to me, a loser
drug addict? I said, "You don't know me man; I am a bad guy." To which
he replied, "I don't care."

The Big Cop showed me Jesus; he loved me like Jesus, unconditionally.

My life was never the same again. I gave my life to Jesus, married that beautiful centerfielder, and never did drugs or alcohol again. I have been doing one-day-at-a-time since July 1, 1973.

If you confess with your mouth that Jesus is Lord and believe in your heart that God raised him from the dead, you will be saved. Romans 10:9

The only way to describe what happened to me is that I was "born again." My encounters first with Joann, then a Big Cop, and then Jesus, changed my life completely and forever. I went from a lost sinner with no hope or future to a forgiven son of God with an incredible adventure ahead alongside of my two most beloved friends, Jesus and Joann.

More Along the Trail

A REAL PLAN

| TJ |

I have never been a big sports guy. The locker room is a foreign place for me. I didn't grow up showering and changing with the team. I never had a locker in the gym. The male camaraderie, towel popping, and all the other guy, team, and player stuff are things I know little about. To be completely honest, they scare me.

In junior high school I refused to dress out in PE. I was embarrassed for some reason. I confused and exasperated my teachers so much that they bought a set of horseshoes to try and get me and a few others to just do something, anything. It was boring; I didn't do it.

Well into adulthood, I was the guy who had a hard time peeing at a urinal and would actually skip relieving myself if that was the only option. Brutal confession, and if it takes a few of my man points away, then so be it.

There are a lot of things, lies from the evil one, that defined me or shaped me along the way. I made a lot of agreements with myself and

Satan. I had no one to teach me how to filter that stuff. I didn't have anyone who would listen and give me feedback.

A lot of guys struggle with the lies the evil one has convinced them are true. Brothers, they are not.

Today I am committed to meeting with men, tearing down the walls, and working to live a life free of the lies I have agreed with for so long. I want to be strong in my faith and strong for my faith. Confessing our struggles is harder than most things a man does to cover up the hurts or fill the gaps. It is easier for far too many men to stay late at work, click on porn, or live in a fantasy about the girl at the office than it is to hold his wife's hands and pray, or talk with his daughter about boys. It's harder to commit to helping at church or a ministry than spending all day Saturday watching sports or any number of other things we do to avoid what really matters.

> "His miseries are his ally; they urge him on. Let them grow, if need be. But do not forsake the secret of life; do not despise those kingly desires. We abandon the most important journey of our lives when we abandon desire. We leave our hearts by the side of the road and head off in the direction of fitting in, getting by, being productive, what have you. Whatever we might gain — money, position, the approval of others, or just absence of the discontent self — it's not worth it." – John Eldredge, *The Journey of Desire: Searching for the Life We Always Dreamed of*

We must have something to fight for. It is who we were made to be. It is core. If you are not in the battle, you are dying. Step in, step up, join, be a part of. You can do this; you are perfectly made for His works—just ask Him.

❤ YOUR HEART TRAIL ❤

So many things make us who we are today. The broken parts, good parts, funny and dangerous parts all encompass our DNA today. What are some of your personal fears? Example: Peeing in a urinal next to another man. Walking in the dark alone. Dying. Losing someone.

What are some of your dreams? No matter the stage of life we find ourselves, we have dreams and desires. For young men it may be building a business or winning at something. For older men it may be joy or legacy. Write down some of yours here.

Therefore encourage one another and build up one another, just as you also are doing. 1 Thessalonians 5:11

DOING IT ONE DAY AT A TIME SINCE APRIL 17, 1986

| TJ |

I really had had enough of it all. I wasn't in a car wreck or jail at the time. I had a job. I was using heavily, but I had improved and wasn't using the harder stuff. But I was tired, real tired. I was going into my mid-to-late twenties; I had a son and a broken marriage. I was offering my son what I got growing up from my dad—no, it was even less. Then I just broke. I wasn't crying or freaking out, I was just willing to do whatever it was going to take.

It was a Tuesday night and just after 7 pm when I got into my car and drove to the church. In the corner of their massive parking lot was a small building with cars, trucks, and people standing around outside. I knew something had to give, something had to change. That's why I was there.

Most of those outside were smoking cigarettes. I parked and walked into the entry area nodding and passing out low volume hellos. I stopped and looked over a table full of informational pamphlets and selected one to read. I found my way into the meeting room full of chairs. I sat down in the back corner, behind a pole.

It was just before 8 pm when a loud rumble drew closer and closer until you could feel it outside the building. Moments later, a group of black leather-clad bikers strode into the room. I tried my best to make myself invisible.

The meeting started on time and there were some ritualistic phrases, a prayer I thought I remembered from Catholic Church, and then folks began talking. It was somewhat structured and topical. Men and women alike began to talk about life without drugs or alcohol. They talked about using and getting loaded. They were open about how hard it could be and how some struggled each day, each moment. There were people there who had gone days, weeks, three months, six months, nine months, even years or multiple years without using. I heard people talking about things I felt and struggles I had in my life. This was all new territory. I was not alone.

After an hour, the guy up front in charge began telling everyone that they could stay clean if they just tried to do it one day at a time, came to meetings, and got a sponsor to help them work their way through the steps. He asked who there was celebrating years, months, days. Then he asked if there was anyone who wanted to try it just one day. So I did. I walked up front, took a key tag, and the girl handing them out gave me a hug.

After the meeting, the biggest of the biker dudes came over to me and wrapped his arms around me and told me he was proud of me. He said, "Get here early for the next ninety days, set up chairs, and stay after to clean ash trays. You can do this." So I did.

That night God began a new chapter in my life. He continues to teach me, show me, and introduce me to a life I had only dreamed of.

Back on that first day when I decided to try and make a change to stay clean, that big ole biker's hug meant the world to me. I was the prodigal son and he accepted me back to life. I so desperately needed that. Today I still need that; I need to be forgiven and accepted back daily.

❤ YOUR HEART TRAIL ❤

Have you ever been addicted? Do you suffer from it today? If not drugs or alcohol, maybe porn, sports, money, work? When we begin to say it out loud, write it, face it, we begin to remove Satan's hold on us and make ourselves available for God. (You may have a need for 12-step recovery or counseling in this area. Talk to someone if you are questioning it.) Begin to expose your struggle here.

_____

_____

_____

_____

_____

If you had written on a piece of paper long ago, what would your biggest dreams have been?

_____

_____

_____

_____

_____

_____

If my people, who are called by my name, will humble themselves and pray and seek my face and turn from their wicked ways, then I will hear from heaven, and I will forgive their sin and will heal their land. Now my eyes will be open and my ears attentive to the prayers offered in this place. 2 Chronicles 7:14-15

So do not fear, for I am with you; do not be dismayed, for I am your God. I will strengthen you and help you; I will uphold you with my righteous right hand. All who rage against you will surely be ashamed and disgraced; those who oppose you will be as nothing and perish. Though you search for your enemies, you will not find them. Those who wage war against you will be as nothing at all. For I am the LORD your God who takes hold of your right hand and says to you, 'Do not fear; I will help you.' Isaiah 41:10-13

CHAPTER 3
BIBLE STUDY

OPENING DISCUSSION
QUESTIONS

Go around the circle and have the men answer one of these questions:

➥ What was one of the Heart Trails that spoke to you?

➥ Do you have regrets for not doing something you wish you would have done earlier in your life as a young man?

➥ Are you a young man fighting today, carrying fear of the unknown?

➥ Are you battling an addiction you want to share today?

LEADER: There are so many trails we can chose during this phase of our life — the early twenties and thirties can be a trying time. It may be that you begin a career, start a family, and build what appears to be a life. It does not have to be burdened. But as a man, we have questions. We are designed to go to battle, build an empire, create a place in the world at this stage, and our being is confused and out-of-order when we **are without a mission**. Society tells us to "relax, hang-out with friends at the beach with a beer, it's all good." But that is not a man's true core being.

You need seasoned men around you who have been through this stage and can tell you of hardships and victories they faced. The battles they fought, won, lost, tied. You should seek their counsel.

BIBLE STUDY
25 minutes

Take turns reading out loud

Joshua in the Young Man Stage

Joshua became Israel's leader at one of the most difficult times in its history. Within days after Moses' death, leadership was assigned to Joshua. He led the nation across the Jordan River into hostile territory and set out to conquer, divide, and settle the "promised" land. It was a daunting task, but Joshua succeeded in this enormous task for some very important reasons.

God's command to Joshua was: *"This is my command—be strong and courageous! Do not be afraid or discouraged. For the Lord your God is with you wherever you go." Joshua 1:9*

Little did Joshua know of the incredible adventure before him, but God knew and commanded him to be a Warrior. He and the nation he led would only survive if they were willing to approach each day as Warriors ready to battle whatever adversary stood in their path.

Joshua had a hunger for God

Exodus 33:7–11

Joshua would accompany Moses to the tent where God talked with Moses face to face. After Moses heard from God, he would leave and address the people. The passage says when Joshua came into the presence of God "he did not leave the tent." Joshua had a deep passion for God that served him well as the Warrior leader.

Joshua had a commitment to obey God

Numbers 13:26-14:9

Of the twelve spies who checked out the land for Moses, only Joshua as a young man and Caleb urged the people to follow God's command and move forward. Forty years later, Joshua was now the leader, obeyed God, and was successful in taking God's Promised Land.

Joshua had Moses as a Mentor

Exodus 24:13, Numbers 11:28

Joshua learned from an older, wiser man about how to be a great leader. Men learn from other men. We learn by watching what they do and then doing the same. This was Jesus' method of teaching the twelve disciples also.

Joshua was a great warrior because he loved God with a great passion and was willing to obey whatever God asked of him, and he knew the value of a Godly man to mentor him.

LESSONS TO LEARN:

➡ Joshua paid attention to what his Godly mentor was doing. He participated.

➡ When God called Joshua up to the task, he stepped forward.

➡ Joshua encouraged others to follow what God was saying, and even though at first many did not, his persistence and example as a leader paid off when he led them into the Promised Land.

APPLICATION
10 minutes

LEADER: Do you know the most viral verse downloaded in the US? Millions of users download this verse every year to get them through the difficult times in life. The verse is *"This is my command, be strong and courageous! Do not be afraid or discouraged. For the Lord your God is with you wherever you go." Joshua 1:9*

The best thing for a young man to have close while building his place in the world is a mentor. For many, to open ourselves up to another man, to allow another guy to see our weaknesses and soft spots, is unthinkable. Our pride, one of Satan's favorite tools (if not his favorite), keeps us to ourselves. It causes us to experience pitfalls and hurts, brokenness and delays, in so many areas of our lives.

 ## CLOSING CONVERSATION

Where are your priorities in your life today? Where are the areas that you feel you most need a trusted advisor? Each man should have three men in their life. An older sage to counsel him on where he is going, a good friend to share the journey with, and a younger one to mentor too along the trail.

We don't have to fight the fight, walk the trail, do this thing alone. No matter the stage of life we are in, we need men in our lives.

Memorize Joshua 1:9: *Be strong and courageous. Do not be afraid; do not be discouraged, for the Lord your God will be with you wherever you go.*

 ## ACTION STEPS

➥ Pick the three men you might have as your three and why.

➥ Ask an older man to coffee. Come with some life questions he can address for you. (You do not age out on this—all guys are challenged here.)

➥ Meet with a friend and do something fun, just two guys.

➥ Do something with a younger guy. Fishing, shooting range, or something exciting.

➥ Write a journal entry to Jesus and ask Him to help you know your place today and how you can best serve Him, care for your family, be a man of God. Build a life based on Him. Ask Him to teach you to hear Him speak.

 **CLOSING PRAYER**

Lord Jesus. Father. Thank you. Thank you for this time together with these other men. Lord, we pray that You reveal to us the places in our hearts that have kept us from becoming closer to You. Our heart's deepest desire is to be the men we long to be. It seems we understand it in our head, but struggle being that man on the outside. We need you Jesus to reveal the ways we can love our wives better. Lord, make us the men worthy of a wife, of the love of an amazing woman. Lord, we so want to share our hearts as men who love You, who can pass on a healthy, God-fearing, Jesus-led example to those in our circles of influence. Open our eyes, break away the lies of the evil one who says we can't do this or don't understand. Lead us, Holy Spirit; our hearts are open, willing, and tender. Make us into the Warriors You want us to be. Amen.

Chapter 4
AS AN ADULT MAN
(30s–40s)

As a young man moves into the adult stage, he may be raising a family. He has fallen in love and it seems different than those before, because it is. This is where he will be taking on responsibilities like a mortgage or important job. He goes to work on time, gets his work done, and becomes a good employee. The man cares for and guides his family. This is a place where a man can thrive. He begins to weigh his choices and decisions because he realizes they matter. He is prime to build a business. He may dive into the things he loves like sports, outdoors, and hobbies. He has to think about his future and what that might look like. He is a man, building his life as a man, leading as a man. He should also be building on the foundation of his faith. He may build churches, ministries, men's groups, and seek an encounter with the Holy Spirit in his walk with Jesus. His faith walk is ready to be built upon at this point. This is a powerful stage for Kingdom work. He will make mistakes, but he is strong and can bounce back. Good, seasoned, Godly, sage mentors are imperative.

SLOWLY IN LOVE

| TJ |

I was building a new business, a landscaping company. We were mowing the grass at commercial buildings and apartment complexes. Getting a call and giving a bid was routine. But there was one day, at one property, the bid would turn out to be anything but routine.

My wife Sandra and I seemed to be absolute opposites in so many ways. She was a young, single, blonde professional; me, a single dad. I was a boot and jeans kinda guy and had a healthy selfish interest in my boy, fishing, and work. I was awarded her property's landscape contract, and that was how we were introduced. I don't think either of us was looking for a relationship at the time. We just worked together. Wayne was my foreman at the time, and he would not quit with the idea that Sandra, "that" property manager, and I should go on a date.

We eventually saw each other at work social events and the idea to date became a thought. Slowly we began to be more intentional about our time together. There were certain things I had committed to that I had to explain to her early on. First, I was a recovering alcoholic and drug addict. I didn't care if she had a drink, but I would not participate. Second, I was on a pause from relationships. I was committed to not being committed to anyone for a year. I had some issues with always feeling like I needed to be connected and I was working on it. Third, I would choose my son and time with him over all things for now. I would probably not invite her around him when I had him. I was just not going to screw up being a dad. She was awesome and honored it all.

When we did have time together, I did things she told me later really made her feel special. Some days I would take her car, get it washed, and fill it with gas. I always opened her door for her. We explored cultural events we both enjoyed. We slowly fell head-over-heals in love.

Our wedding day was a blur. She had done an exceptional job as our wedding planner. I remember her turning inside the door to walk down the aisle. She was and is the most beautiful woman I have ever seen. I wept from deep inside, knowing that she was truly the right woman God had for me. I remember sitting in the seats after the ceremony writing checks to all the vendors, pastor, and photographer, and realizing when we got back from the honeymoon that she would come to the house, and never leave. Things got real, fast. That night in the hotel room before flying to Italy, we ordered pizza and watched Cops on TV. We laugh about that to this day. The perfect night even now, years later.

As a step-mom, she invited my son into her heart. I never felt she did not love, care for, and accept him. She became friends with his mom — weird for me but over the years it was a huge blessing. Our two kids followed soon after we were married. One really cool thing we did was that we held off knowing if it was a boy or a girl until the moment God gave them to us. It was and is one of the most incredible moments, face to face with God in human birth. Wow.

Early on, we tried to leave the kids at daycare while she worked. Dr. Laura, the radio personality, was on the talk radio station every day and she was adamant about moms staying home and raising their kids, at any cost. It became increasingly emotional and convicting for us. So Sandra quit her job and worked from home. She has been, and is, the best example of a mom I could have prayed for. She took the kids to the park, made lunch, invited every stray kid to our home for love and food and games. Watching her mother our kids has been a joy.

And all the time along the way, she based her wife and mothering duties on old-school principles. She always allowed me to work long hours and care for the family as I needed. She would clean the house and light a candle before I came home. I was and am always greeted with a smile and a joyful hug and kiss. She loves our home.

Marriage can be hard. Learning to give it all for another, to give them what they want or need over our personal desires and wants. Selfishness can be a brutal mistress in marriage. I want to jump off a building in marital frustration on some days. I am sure she would push me off that same building on some days. But we are both committed to try and work through it all.

I can be as mean as an old house cat. I can find my interests distracting me from "us." My heart longs to be one kind of guy, yet I act out as another. Some days, I see in who I am the examples I got from my dad. But those things are not okay to blame as the reason I fail at loving my wife well today. The key for me today is that I have to fight to do better. It takes work. I have to be intentional about pursuing my wife and changing who I have been. As men, that is our calling.

The best advice we got in our premarital counseling that stuck with me was, "Never say divorce, or I am leaving, or why don't you leave."

Never. In my past, all relationships were optional. If things got rough, I left. Simple. The fruit of a good marriage, leading with Jesus, being a strong father, husband, man, is a legacy I want to leave. I believe she is here to stay and so am I. That is as long as I don't get her mad while standing near the edge of a tall building.

LEARNING WHAT IT MEANS TO REALLY LOVE

| JOE DON |

The four most significant days of my life are the day I came to Christ, the day I married Joann, and the birth of my daughter and my son. Each one of these dates was forever life changing.

So now I enter a season of life filled with a family looking to me to provide for and protect them. I am all grown up and life is filled with a lot of responsibility. A job, a home, bills to pay, a wife to learn to love, and kids to raise.

I knew how to be selfish and self-centered, but I was clueless in how to love a wife and kids. I certainly had no role models. I wanted to do what was right and I would have to learn on my own. I turned to my new favorite book, the Bible.

The simple definition of God found in the Bible is that He is love. What attracted me to Him was His unconditional love for me. He loved me even though I was a mess. I began the journey of learning to love myself and others without conditions. I eliminated the phrase, "I will love you if..."

My focus was on my family. After growing up in such a dysfunctional home, I wanted my own family to be different. Every day I prayed, "God I need your help raising these kids. I do not want to screw them up like my parents did me."

Let me share with you a few thoughts from this time in my life.

I can honestly say, "Where have the years gone?" I heard a wise person say, "The days were hard, but the years were short." I would agree—while in the midst of child rearing you think the kids will never grow up. When parenting gets to be overwhelming, you look forward to the day when they will finally be "launched" into their own lives and you will finally get to enjoy an empty nest. Hooray, no more kids. But then you realize the years are short and the baby of the family has grown up and has his own Dodge pickup and doesn't need you much anymore. You look forward to that day, until it comes.

You realize you too have grown older and that what was important to you then is not as important anymore. What is important now is, have I done a good job of preparing my kids for life? We know how hard life can be. Will they find a Godly mate to grow old with? Will they be able to support a family, marry a man who can? Most of all, will they be a family of faith in God?

Have I invested the time in my marriage and kids to help mold them into who God wants them to be? Or was I too busy with work or my hobbies? Was it all about me or was it all about them?

Teaching involves both words and actions. A Godly life is lived out. Our kids learn from their daddy by watching what he does and not just what he says. Our wives know we love them by showing them with our actions and words.

When I was delivering my son to college in California, we had an 18-hour drive together, just me and my boy. My heart was heavy hoping I had prepared him for life without the protection of Dad and Mom. He was now a young man. I told him I wish I had spent more time with him reading the Bible together, and he said something that brings tears to my eyes many years later. "I have watched you Dad and I know what is important to you."

What would your son say is "most important to you?" Please listen to me, men with sons and daughters, don't be deceived into the lie of, "I spend quality time with my kids and not quantity time." It is both.

Those who are wise will find a time and a way to do what is right." Ecclesiastes 8:5

Your challenge as a man of God, a husband, and a father is to keep the main thing the main thing. It is all about loving God, loving your wife like Jesus loves her, and loving and leading your family well. You must be intentional with your time; it just won't happen on its own.

More Stories
Along the Trail

POT SCRUBBER

| TJ |

There are certain things that, as a man, I feel required to do or be responsible for around the house. When the toilet gets clogged up, I get the call. When the yard has branches or fencing problems, it is mine. Most of these things my wife or kids could do, but they are left to me because they are my job. All that is fine because I like accomplishing things; I like working in the yard then sitting back and looking at the results—many times with a cigar in hand.

My wife has certain things she does that are hers. There are things that she does not want me to touch—she hates the way I fold things. Honestly, I am okay with her "keep your hands off" approach. She needs to keep away from my grill and chain saw, so there. She likes to clean the house. She likes dusting and spraying cleaners and organizing. She will tell you it is therapeutic with a smile on her face. I want her to be happy.

Before we got married, I kept an impeccable house. I was ultra-organized, had the laundry done nightly, cooked and cleaned with gusto. It seems not long after we were married those skill sets began to wane, then continued a downward spiral to almost nothing. I never intentionally meant to turn over the cleaning and laundry to my wife, it just happened. Don't misunderstand, I still get asked to help and those times I get asked, I better perform. There are consequences.

There was a period in my life when I spent a lot of time listening to motivational speakers. I had a handful whom I really enjoyed and got me fired up. Motivational speakers can be very positive influences in your life, and if you were to pick up on any one lesson, chances are you would grow personally or in business. The two I really enjoyed the most were Brian Tracy and Zig Ziglar.

Brian Tracy really taught me some skills when it comes to selling and professional relationships. I must have worn out two cassette tape series (for you young guys they were a thing before digital) listening to them over and over in my truck. He also taught me how to be organized and efficient with my time.

Zig Ziglar is my favorite because he uses wonderful personal stories and visual aids to get his point across. For years, he carried around a big chrome hand water pump that he would get to cranking up and down to demonstrate a point that I can't remember.

I do remember one thing specific that Zig did say and I began implementing with conviction. It is not a sales tool or a marketing angle, not really. Zig said he never lets his wife wash the big pots and pans. If she used a big frying pan, stew pot, or anything big like that, he hand-washed it, dried it, and put it away. He was adamant about this.

I started to do this at our house. It can really be a drag on some days. Recently when my wife very lovingly put something in the oven to warm up for dinner, she forgot there was a plastic tray under the foil. The house filled with smoke and the plastic dripped and covered all the racks and bottom of the oven. I rushed in as she worried about the fire and mess. I immediately began the clean-up process that took several hours but resulted in a sparkling clean oven. I guess the oven is a giant pot of sorts anyway.

I know I can always do a little more to help around the inside of the house. This one little gesture, cleaning the pots, has been unspoken to date, but then I am not doing it for a pat on the back or a thank you. I need—I want—to be a good husband and the knight in shining armor for my biggest cheerleader. We have a joke around our house that the sock fairy always delivers clean socks right before my sock drawer is empty. Now I am not one who believes in fairy tales and the like, but that one is one I want to continue to believe in. If it takes getting to that mystical land of clean and wonderful smelling laundry by including a few scrubbed pots, a broom, or other inside chores on my side of the list, I'm in.

❤ YOUR HEART TRAIL ❤

Do you have responsibilities that you were once good at keeping up with but slacked up on now? Did you used to jump right up to take out the trash or lower the seat in the bathroom but now maybe not? As a single guy, what are some of your good habits? Example: I mow the lawn every other Saturday. I keep my house and car clean. I love to cook for people.

List a few things here you once did but maybe not so much now. Remind yourself.

_____

_____

_____

_____

_____

Are you selfish with your time? Do you strive to give back more than you want or expect to get? Where are some places you are all about you? Where do you give back? List both.

_____

_____

_____

_____

_____

Likewise, husbands, live with your wives in an understanding way, showing honor to the woman as the weaker vessel, since they are heirs with you of the grace of life, so that your prayers may not be hindered. 1 Peter 3:7

I have been crucified with Christ. It is no longer I who live, but Christ who lives in me. And the life I now live in the flesh I live by faith in the Son of God, who loved me and gave himself for me. Galatians 2:20

WHAT ARE TWENTY-TWO MINUTES WORTH?

| TJ |

There is not a lot you can do in just twenty-two minutes. It's not long enough to watch a TV show, and you can't drive hardly anywhere, or make it through the checkout stand at a busy grocery. I can get dressed and out the door in that time, but my wife? Not a chance. Most people connecting to their Facebook page, talking on the phone, or checking email go over twenty-two minutes easily. What are twenty-two minutes worth, anyway? The average person worldwide lives about 64.3 years. This would be 33,819,228 minutes; what can possibly come from only twenty-two minutes of that?

I once asked a friend of mine who was coming off cancer treatment if he wanted to take a weekend and go with me fishing; he said no. He told me how he only had a certain number of Saturdays until his son was 18 (he gave me the exact number), and said that he really did not like to miss any of them. Wow, that really took me off balance. How could someone be so in tune with their life, their time left here? It had to be the reality that came with knowing that he could go at any time, that his cancer could have taken him out of his son's life. Can a regular person, who does not fear imminent death or a tragic event, come to the same realization?

God spoke to me that day. I realized that one of the things that I considered a hassle, driving my then 14-year-old to school each day, needed to be looked at differently. As the youngest and only one left at home, my son would in just two years walk out to his own vehicle and drive himself to school. I needed to change my way of experiencing mornings with him. God pressed in on me; I was not sure what it should look like, but I knew that somehow those twenty-two minutes a day had to matter more.

For the next two years I was there to drive him, and then to drive with him when he got his learner's permit. No matter how late my travels brought me home, I was standing at the front door, ready to roll, in the morning. At first we would just talk, and then I started reading a daily devotional. It was all good but it never felt just right. Then we found *The Knight's Code* by Robert Noland, and began to take turns reading it on the way, and talking about what we read. We designated the last stretch of the drive a "prayer road" and prayed each day for a good day and more.

Now, it was not always some pretty, Spirit-filled sanctuary in that truck. Not by a long shot. We took turns being really crap-heads to each other, and on the days we were both that way, well, look out. But for the most part I think it made a difference; at least it did to me. We talked about some serious topics and had a few really good moments where I felt God's presence.

Eventually we found an old Dodge pickup. It was a good deal and fit what our vision and our budget could handle for his first truck. Then the day came—I walked him to the end of the drive and watched as he loaded that old Dodge pickup with his baseball gear, his backpack, and his lunch, and then he drove off, alone, to school. I was awash in emotions.

As the days crept by, I could not help wonder if there was anything, anything at all, that he took away from our morning commute time together. One day he volunteered to drive me to the store to get some things his mom needed. As we drove along, I noticed he had a towel on the console between the seats and a pack of baby wipes in the slot on his driver's door. Those were things I have always done in my truck, for years. I had to wonder: if he picked up on that, what else did he get? Did he hear the part about keeping God first, keeping a good band of brothers close, truth, honor, and respect?

After he began driving himself, I had to figure out what to do with that twenty-two minutes each morning. I tried going to the gym, which I did not like. I started running at the park, which I do like. It's amazing, that time has kept me focused in the mornings. I struggle on days I don't get my morning time, at least twenty-two minutes. Thanks son.

♥ YOUR HEART TRAIL ♥

What was something someone did for you that looking back now was intentional or a burden they took on to help you? Something selfless. Example: My uncle always took me hunting with my cousins. My neighbor mowed my yard when I was out of town each summer.

_____

_____

_____

_____

What can you do to give of yourself to someone else? Sacrificial love is a huge blessing. Do something that you don't say anything about to anyone. Do it anonymously.

_____

_____

_____

_____

CHAPTER 4
BIBLE STUDY

OPENING DISCUSSION QUESTIONS _15 minutes_

Go around the circle and have the men answer one of these questions:

➡ What was one of the Heart Trails that spoke to you?

➡ How do you hear from God and have you heard from Him this week?

➡ If you are a single guy, where is your heart in all of this?

_____

BIBLE STUDY
25 minutes

Take turns reading out loud.

God the Father

Joe Don shared about his dad dying in a car wreck when he was a little boy. He felt abandoned and alone with no one to guide him along the trails of life. He stumbled along having to make all his own decisions and failing often. He grew up independent and self-sufficient. There was no one to rely on. He thought, "I must do it myself." A boy needs a father to love him, lead him, teach him how to love his wife, kids, and others.

God loved us enough to create us:

Then God said, 'Let us make mankind in our image, in our likeness, so that they may rule over the fish in the sea and the birds in the sky, over the livestock and all the wild animals, and over all the creatures that move along the ground. Genesis 1:26

We all know the story of how Adam and Eve sinned and were cast out of Paradise and their relationship was affected, but God still loved them as He loves us.

God's love is forever faithful:

Know therefore that the Lord your God is God; He is the faithful God, keeping His covenant of love to a thousand generations of those who love Him and keep His commandments. Deuteronomy 7:9

God instructs us as a Father:

I have set before you life and death, blessings and curses. Now choose life, so that you and your children may live and that you may love the Lord your God, listen to His voice, and hold fast to Him. For the Lord is your life, and He will give you many years in the land. Deuteronomy 30:19, 20

God's love protects us:

How priceless is your unfailing love, O God! People take refuge in the shadow of your wings. Psalm 36:7

Nothing can separate us from God's love:

No, in all these things we are more than conquerors through Him who loved us. For I am convinced that neither death nor life, neither angels nor demons, neither the present nor the future, nor any powers, neither height nor depth, nor anything else in all creation, will be able to separate us from the love of God that is in Christ Jesus our Lord. Romans 8:37-39

God loves sinners:

But God demonstrates his own love for us in this: While we were still sinners, Christ died for us. Romans 5:8

God's love gave us Jesus to die for us:

For God so loved the world that He gave His one and only Son, that whoever believes in Him shall not perish but have eternal life. John 3:16

LESSONS TO LEARN:

➡ God planned us, every hair on our head, every day, every breath, before time.

➡ God's love is never conditional or wavering.

➡ God forgives us for years ago, yesterday, today, and tomorrow.

➡ God gave us His Son. The ultimate sacrifice. He gave Him to us because we were weak but He is strong. A true example of love.

APPLICATION
10 minutes

LEADER: Life is full of distractions and they just keep getting worse, unless you are intentional about removing them. You have to be intentional about every important area of your life if you want it to be successful and flourish.

The world tells us emails need to be checked as soon as you get out of bed. If you do not reply fast enough, you lose. The evil one is in distractions.

The world tells us if we don't let our kids play baseball on the team on Sunday, we are setting them up to fail; we are irresponsible. Our ego and pride keep us out of church—oh how the evil one loves that.

Following Jesus is counter-intuitive to the world's definition of success. Taking time to read your Bible, spending good time with your wife and kids, and making church a priority can seem a burden. But when you make Him your priority, you will see a huge change and the blessing that comes with it.

Every fast food chain operator would tell you they can never close on a Sunday, it will destroy the business. But the one that does, Chick-fil-a, is the most profitable one in America. Not what the world would tell you. God's currency is time and love.

Our wives desperately seek our love and attention, even if they do not express it.

Do you love your wife and kids unconditionally like God loves you? Do you understand unconditional? Definition of unconditional: not conditional or limited.

CLOSING DISCUSSION
5 minutes

For some of us expressing love can be a hurdle we must face. We may not have been taught what it was or how to express it, but God really does offer it to us. It will require us to scrub some pots, be intentional about our 22-minute times, invest in our kids and marriage today. Where is the evil one telling you that you can't make a change, but your heart, wife, or kids are begging you to? You know this, you feel it. Write them down.

_____

_____

_____

_____

_____

_____

 ACTION STEPS

➥ On Saturday morning get up early, go wash your wife's car, fill it with gas. Don't expect anything in return, just do it.

➥ Help someone who needs it. Mow their grass, tip a waitress well, volunteer where you are not in charge. Selfless random acts of kindness, intentionally not looking for recognition.

➥ Where are your 22-minute places? Where can you turn a hassle or a regular meeting into a blessing? Plan time away with your wife, your son or daughter, a visit to your parents or grandparents or a friend. Make it a time where you are intentional to spend that time with them. Create a memory. Learn to listen and not react. Turn off all electronics.

 **CLOSING PRAYER**

But God demonstrates his own love for us in this: While we were still sinners, Christ died for us. Romans 5:8

Lord, please teach me to be a lover like You. Heal the wounded lover in me. Forgive me of all my sins and failures. I want to love people unconditionally like my Father in Heaven.

Recite the Lord's Prayer out loud.
(Note Jesus instructs us to call God "Father.")

Our Father in heaven, hallowed be Your name,
Your kingdom come,
Your will be done, on earth as it is in heaven.
Give us today our daily bread.
And forgive us our debts as we also have forgiven our debtors.
And lead us not into temptation,
but deliver us from the evil one.
Amen

Chapter 5
RISING AS A LEADER OF MEN
(40s–50s)

As a man in the world, he now has his place. This is usually the most powerful time in a man's life. At this point a guy should know about working. He is in a place at work where he makes decisions that affect others. He may have built a business and is enjoying the fruits of owning his own business. His kids have left home for college and are getting married. Grandkids become part of the picture. His voice is heard when he speaks because he has proven himself to be a good steward of his home, his family, and his relationships. He leads in his church with his activities there and his desire to make a difference. He has learned to tithe and give. He has learned to hear from God, talk to God, listen for God. He may begin to realize that he needs to step even deeper into his relationship with his wife. He realizes that honoring her is honoring God, and it matters.

MOUNTAIN TOPS AND MEANING

| TJ |

As a teen and young twenty-something, I roamed the streets. I had three things I found training and acceptance in. The sales, manufacturing, and distribution of illegal chemical and agricultural products (drugs). I left that line of work once I realized it would cause serious interruption in my life if I ever got caught. Prison tends to do that. My heart was also tormented with the hurt and the destruction that lifestyle created. Sobering up, having asked Jesus into my heart, my son coming along, and the prompting of the Holy Spirit all finally had me beginning to think about what I was going to do for work.

Construction. There were homes and apartment complexes being built everywhere. This was a guy's world and I learned to work hard on the job. Hot, cold, rain, dark, tired, none of it mattered if the boss said we were working. If I was on a construction job, I never just carried one or two boards; I carried eight or ten. Never walk, run. Always look busy. My bosses would complement me on my hard work and hustle, so I worked harder and faster. I soaked up being among men and being acknowledged.

Multi-family homes. I found that apartments would hire me first as a porter, then make-ready, then full-fledged maintenance man. I learned to get there early, on the first day or two straighten up the maintenance rooms, closets, and shops. Be polite and respectful. The great thing about the apartment work in those days was that they offered a free apartment with the job. That was a huge motivator for me as a young man. The managers liked me and treated me really well when I was working hard for them. I tried to never let them down.

As I learned the construction and maintenance trades, I began to get asked to do little side projects that people would pay me to do. Mistakes and failures trained me in the school of hard knocks. But I kept at it. In a lot of ways, I had no choice—I had to work or I would not eat. I see now all the mentors God introduced me to who trained me in crafts, skills, and trades.

Eventually I had enough side work that if I kept at it, I could go it on my own. Early mornings and late into the night doing any job I could was a key. Building a business was a dream come true. I listened to motivational speakers, went to sales seminars, found retired executives to train me in bookkeeping and business structure. I read books on mergers and takeovers, corporate executives and their companies. I loved the Wall Street Journal and Zig Ziglar. I had no formal background, but that did not seem to matter if I worked hard and was honest.

I built a construction company with dozens of employees and job sites across the country. It was exciting for me to travel and see my guys working. I continued to learn; the money was good; the freedom was great; my family lacked for nothing.

After getting married, my wife had an idea we turned into a business. A directory for apartment managers to find contractors. Of course, the publishing business. I never thought too much about it, we just started it. Then a music magazine came out of that endeavor. Our graphic artist from the directory suggested we start a country music magazine. Of course we should, so we did. After we partnered with a country radio station, they asked what we would like—a radio show of course. They said okay.

Then one day I began to notice that my drive to build this large construction, landscape business began to fade. I wasn't sure what God was doing. It made no sense to a bootstrap, make-it-happen guy like me. One December day, after I had logged in the best year ever for the construction business, God said, "Stop." I argued with Him. "Whoa there, Sir, I can't do that. "Stop." I can't explain how or why I conformed to such a request, except that God walked me through it. I took all the tools out of my truck and that was it.

By this time, I was doing the beginnings of what would become the Kids Outdoor Zone (KOZ) ministry. It wasn't meant to be more than a few guys doing good works with the kids we knew. I had rallied my buddies from church to help with my Sunday school class of third through fifth grade boys. These guys and the boys from the neighborhood all rolled into one Saturday a month outings we eventually called KOZ. I thrived on the planning and creating what the Saturday would look like. We realized the impact we were having on the boys and became intentional about sharing Jesus and outdoor skills. We started to do weekend hunting, fishing, and camping trips.

My wife and I sold the directories. The country music, lifestyle magazine slowed way down and went online. The radio show was fun and we kept it; it flourished. For me, however, everything became a tool for ministry and outreach.

When I was offered to lead a media department at a large outdoor retailer, I hit my knees. I had never felt worthy of anything at that level. Not this high school dropout with a history. My wife and I agreed it was a gift from God and I should take the job. It would offer our family a foundation with insurance, retirement, and a new home in a great community near Houston, Texas.

I was away from home a lot and had to disconnect from everything I knew. No coaching, no men's group, no church, no Bible study. We packed a lot of the kids' stuff and put our home up for sale. Eleven months and five days into the job, I was let go. What in the world was that, God?

It was not long after, with the help of my mentors, we realized what God had done. While I was away, my buddies kept the Saturday KOZ events going with our boys. Each month I worked on the script for them to use while I was away. I also wrote out why we did it. If I was not going to be there, they needed the whole story and plan in one place. Over that eleven months and five days, I had written an 80-page training manual and curriculum. God had taken me out of my busyness to a still, quiet place where I could write the ministry plan for KOZ.

Then God said to give it away to any man in any church who wanted it. A few buddies at local churches used it and it took off. Then we had a chance to train a guy in West Virginia, and it worked at his church. Soon after, God introduced us to a large men's conference in Lynchburg, Virginia, and 150 men asked for more information. We launched KOZ around the US and Canada after that.

Jesus used all the things I loved as a kid. My heart for the outdoors, adventure, boy's stuff. He used the broken pieces of a lost boy wandering the streets. He used the desire to build a business into the building of a ministry. My life has been a training ground for what I am doing today. Every broken and joyful moment.

I guess if anyone asked, "What is it you want to do?" I would have to say I am doing it. It's not what I thought it would be all those years ago, it's better. I still love the smell of fresh cut lumber and building things. Working with the Master Carpenter Jesus is more than I could have ever imagined.

THE PATH TO A LIFETIME DREAM

| JOE DON |

Twenty years after my high school graduation, I went back to Midland, Texas, to my high school reunion. Everything had changed so much since that season of life. Everyone had grown up into men and women with families and careers. Not one of us became what we thought we would have been when we were 18 years old. My dream of being a professional basketball player fell way "short" (forgive the pun).

We were each asked to stand and announce what we did for a living. I sat patiently as many followed their fathers into the family oil business, some doctors, others lawyers, homemakers, etc.

When it was finally my turn, I stood and announced, "I am a pastor of a church." The room gasped in disbelief. As many would share with me afterwards, I would have been selected the "least likely to become a pastor" in my entire senior class in 1968.

Like I said, a lot had changed since those days. I hit the bottom after years of experiencing the sex, drugs, and rock and roll of the 60s. I met Joann and Jesus and it changed everything. My life became totally devoted to following Jesus and loving and leading my family.

I felt "called" by God to enter the ministry and began an intensive season of preparation in furthering my education in Bible College and Seminary.

My first opportunity to be a Senior Pastor was at the little Baptist church in Denver where I met Jesus and Joann. They had experienced a split and only 25 people remained. I served there five years and grew the church to 125 people. I was worn out emotionally, burning the candle at both ends with seminary, 60 hour a week work schedule at Rocky Mountain News, preaching three sermons a week, and raising my family.

I resigned and felt I had missed the call, maybe I just *thought* I had heard God's voice. I felt like a failure as a pastor and left the ministry.

We changed churches to a brand new church plant with a young, dynamic pastor and lots of young families like ours. My family soaked it all in and healed. We were enjoying sitting in the audience minding our own business when the young pastor convinced me to come on as his part-time Associate Pastor. Reluctantly, I accepted.

Two years after re-entering the ministry the young pastor fell morally and I was selected to become the new Senior Pastor. All of my life stories of losing my dad as a little boy, being raised by an alcoholic step-father, failing to win a scholarship, crashing in the 60s, meeting Joann and Jesus, becoming a fully devoted follower of Christ, saying "yes" to God's call, and feeling like I failed in ministry prepared me for that time in my life. I was now ready to lead. Everything finally made sense. The old saying of "whatever doesn't kill you makes you stronger" was true in my life. Hardship had molded me into the man God wanted me to be.

The next 13 years of my life were powerful. People said the church would "die" losing the founding pastor, but a band of warriors along with God said "over our dead bodies." We watched God do amazing things in and through Foothills Community Church in Denver, Colorado. The church grew from 200 to over 2,000 people and the stories of lives and marriages being restored are too many to even count.

I never thought I would ever be the leader of such an amazing church. Foothills far exceeded any of my expectations. How could God have done such an amazing thing with such a flawed leader with a past filled with hardships and failures?

That is what God does. He takes the weak to do things that require strength. He takes the fearful to do acts of courage. He takes failures and makes them champions.

Our God is the God of second and third and fourth chances. He wants to do the miraculous in and through you. The path to my lifetime dream was really hard, but worth it all.

MEN OF HONOR

| TJ |

Honor all men, love the brotherhood, fear God,
honor the King.
1 Peter 2:17

I love that Scripture. It brings up something inside me, a young warrior spirit, a sense of honor, a desire to do good. I have always felt that way but, alas, I have not always acted that way. Even in my heart where I deeply desire to be one kind of person, I fail miserably and become another.

In 1 Peter chapter two, Peter talks about how we are to react regarding politics. So much is going on right now and Satan is loving it. If you are a believer, you are given specific direction on how you are to react at times like these.

The important thing above all else is how we portray ourselves as the Christian men that we are. How do we act and what do we say in those political conversations or in public forums, especially if you are a leader in your church?

The Bible tells us we are to be an example. Our tongue can do more damage than our swords. In our righteousness, we exclaim the need for all those around us to assume our position. There may be justification in the ideals and thoughts you want to share but think this through.

As men, we are charged with training up the next generation. Back in the day, the boys were trained under the father. Dad would head out to work the fields and the son would follow as the morning light crept over the horizon. The boys learned by watching and with their hands on the plow, rock bar, and hammer. The boys followed their uncle into the woods and trained as a hunter. They were sent next door to help Farmer Brown milk his cows.

It was in those moments between chores, as they walked, the adult male would share the words of wisdom he was to bestow on the boy. "Money buys everything but good sense." "Deal with the faults of others as gently as your own." "Lost time is never found again."

Statistics show recent protests and rioting include a large proportion of the fatherless. You will not hear that on the news. Society would have to take a big look at itself if it confessed its failure to the fatherless. The big, pink elephant in the room is today's culture, one that does not honor the male role model. The boys are not being trained how to handle themselves. They operate from their masculine drive—battle, mission, and action, but it is misdirected and without honor. I would bet if you had the chance to spend a few days in the woods with most of these young men, they would think differently when they emerged.

If you teach and live the message of the Bible, you will be honoring God as His living examples. Be careful how you express your political convictions. We are to live by a different standard. Honor that.

♥ YOUR HEART TRAIL ♥

What are some words, comments, or attitudes that you were taught or you heard as a boy that caused you to form opinions in your mind and heart about something such as racism, pride, lust, etc.? Do you now, as an adult man and believer, see things through a different lens? Note a few here.

_____

_____

_____

_____

If you are a politic-watching, electronic-feed-of-news, always-tuning-in kind of guy, try tuning out. Leave all politics, television, talk radio, cable, and online news feeds out of your head for one week. Ask God what it is He wants you to see or think about in that time of fasting. Talk to Him. List some things He may be saying.

_____

_____

_____

_____

_____

Do not let any unwholesome talk come out of your mouths, but only what is helpful for building others up according to their needs, that it may benefit those who listen. Ephesians 4:29

First of all, then, I urge that supplications, prayers, intercessions, and thanksgivings be made for all people, for kings and all who are in high positions, that we may lead a peaceful and quiet life, godly and dignified in every way. 1 Timothy 2:1-2

RAISING A SON @ 14,000 FEET

| TJ |

The interstate was not very crowded at 6 am on a Sunday. We traveled a couple hundred miles until we really saw any traffic, and even then the long open road ahead had plenty of room for everyone going west. This was going to be the longest drive we had had to experience on our father/son quest to scale America's top twelve peaks.

My son Jon-Michael was 17 at the time, I was 56, and I felt the need to get this done. Mount Whitney is the tallest peak in the lower 48 at 14,505 ft. This was our fifth peak. Over the years we have taken on one peak each summer. Texas, New Mexico, Arizona, and Colorado. Each peak is a "do hard things" experience in its own right. Each high point has been beautiful and powerful, hard and deeply satisfying to our male souls.

As a dad, especially the dad of a teen, there are so many distractions. The world today seems to be spinning faster than ever before. For the parent, there are interferences and obligations at work that don't seem to conclude after punching the time clock at 5 pm. Social media is a distraction plaguing the attention of our kids. If we are honest, lots of adults are sucked into it as well. Recent studies tell us kids spend on average forty minutes a week outside and seventy hours a week looking at a screen, and as adults we are not far behind.

Boys begin to separate from their mom in their mid to late teens and struggle for independence and personal identity. They want to be a man; they want to test their wings and try to find out if they have what it takes. This is where Dad has to be vigilant. The boy wants to hear he has what it takes from a man. For Jon-Michael and me, we chose the mountains to help answer his questions.

You do have to be in good shape, as any good hike or summit can take you. Jon-Michael was a thin, strong 17-year-old who did not need much preparation. His biggest struggle was to eat well and drink lots and lots of water. He knew the struggles of altitude and had learned to combat it up front. Even with his good health and preparation, the altitude was noticeable. Mount Whitney was harder on me than any of the other peaks so far. Lightheadedness, fatigue, aches, and pains from the hike and altitude were more defined this time. Overall, water was the biggest asset, and we drank a lot.

Our transportation was a Dodge Grand Caravan. So you're thinking, "Ha, those guys took a minivan." Well, I guess that is what most folks would call it. We found it to be the Premium Adventure Travel Vehicle, or as we extreme adventurers call it, a PATV. All the seats folded down into the floor to give us great space for gear and resting while on the road. The ride was like silk. The PATV had lots of power and could get onto the freeway and down the road with the best of them. It had all the luxuries you could ask for, including flip down video, satellite radio, and massive a/c system.

Mount Whitney requires a permit to hike and camp. Most recommendations tell you to get into the lottery well in advance, say in the spring. I heard the chance for a walk up was good during the week, and I was praying for that. I knew we could cross over into Nevada and hit the tallest peak there, Boundary Peak (on our list), but we wanted to do Mount Whitney first, and were willing to wait it out a day or two.

I was up early and over to the ranger station before 8 am. Problem was, I went to the wrong station. I was five minutes late when I got to the correct one. I took a number and by the time I was called, all leftover permits were gone. It would be 11 am before the next drawing, if any were available, and so I went back to camp. We packed up and found a local diner where we devoured some high-carb pancakes in anticipation of getting our permits or taking a long nap. We were back at the station at 10:45 and at exactly 11:00 they handed out numbers again. Crud, I got number nine. It didn't matter; we got the permits—the last two for that day. Yes.

We headed up to the beginning of the trailhead and packed our final gear into our backpacks. Mine weighed in at 37 lbs. JM's was about 25. Heavy, but not too heavy. We arrived at base camp at 10,000 feet four hours into the hike. It was late afternoon, but plenty of light and time to set up and relax. It was magnificent. Waterfalls, clear streams, cool temperatures. We ate potato soup and granola for dinner. Neither of us was too hungry. The altitude was messing with us a bit. We bunked out just after dark. I had a small western paperback, random mindless reading, but had left it in the truck. That night the hours crept by and rest was fleeting.

It was 5:30 am when we saw lights outside the tent. Hikers start from the base at 2:00 or 2:30 for single day hikes. It is brutal and I do not recommend it. It can be done and is a lot, but you can miss a whole lot of beauty. Again, it can be done. We were up quick, strapped on our day packs for the summit hike, and took off. The sun was already breaking away the darkness when we left camp.

It was 12:30 when we peaked out. The trail at the very top was icy and worn through a layer of snow-covered scree and mud. There in front of us was the stone summit hut, built in the early 1900s, that we had seen in so many pictures. It was an emotional moment for us. Jon-Michael kept repeating, "We are here." We took pictures. Stood in awe of the cloud lines that circled the edge of the peak. We ate a bit and enjoyed a few minutes contemplating where we were.

When we finally rolled back into the parking lot, it was still light. We tossed our gear into the back of the PATV, not very concerned about the organization of it all. On the way down from the top, we had one big motivator: a giant pizza and a hotel room with good beds. Our day ended well and sleep came easy.

The drive back home included additional elements of adventure, but for the most part the task had been completed; our hearts were full, our bodies sore, and thoughts of home were comforting. I loved the conversations about what was ahead for him in his life and hearing his thoughts. I loved the still, quiet moments when Jesus was there with us. I love when Jon-Michael allows me to mentor him and share from my heart.

So far, the trail to the top of these peaks with JM has been one of the highlights of my life. I never considered climbing all these peaks, but I am loving it. We need to have things in our lives that challenge us, stretch us, and confirm us. Jon-Michael has done some powerful things in his young life. Hopefully one day down the road he will be faced with something hard, remember climbing those peaks with his old man, and hearing my voice in his head, "Hydrate son, hydrate," and push right on through.

♥ YOUR HEART TRAIL ♥

Do you have goals or plans laid out ahead of you? Write out a few goals you would like to consider. Things to do alone, with others, your wife, kids, or friends. Be realistic and crazy.

_____

_____

_____

_____

_____

What is something hard that you are facing? Health issues, older parents, job change? Write some things you are facing now or will face in the future.

_____

_____

_____

_____

_____

Blessed is the man who remains steadfast under trial, for when he has stood the test he will receive the crown of life, which God has promised to those who love him. James 1:12

The plans of the diligent lead surely to abundance, but everyone who is hasty comes only to poverty. Proverbs 21:5

 # CHAPTER 5
BIBLE STUDY

 ## OPENING DISCUSSION
QUESTIONS *15 minutes*

Go around the circle and have the men answer one of these questions:

➥ What was one of the Heart Trails that spoke to you?

➥ Can you define a desire you feel and long for?

➥ Have you asked Jesus into your mountaintop dreams? If not, why?

LEADER: This season of a man's life should be good. We have built ourselves a work base or job profile. We have older kids and our marriages are settled in. Not everything is perfect of course, but good. It is critical we have a few things that are foundational as well. Our walk with Jesus should be healthy and growing. We should also understand our hearts. What a man is, what a man does, what our purpose for God is in this life. Again, we should have good counsel and good friends.

 ## BIBLE STUDY
25 minutes

David in the Leader Stage

Still to this day David is considered the greatest King in Israel's long history. He certainly had great accomplishments, but it is more than that. It is the story of his lifetime that inspires men and women today as it did in the days he was leading Israel.

David's preparation at this time in his life was to become a leader of men, a King over others.

David came from humble roots. He was the eighth and youngest son of Jesse. His job in the family was nothing more than shepherd to the sheep. A thankless job, but one in which God had used to develop other great leaders like Moses. God is not looking for perfect people.

David was anointed as future King as a teenager.
(Read I Samuel 16:7–13 out loud.)

The most famous battle in the Old Testament was not between two armies, but between two people. It was between a warrior giant named Goliath, who stood 9' 9" tall and was a seasoned killing machine, and a young teenage boy named David, armed only with a slingshot, five small stones, and yes, God.

Read 1 Samuel 17:32–51 (out loud).

We can define the lessons David learned in this book. As a young boy, facing a giant had to be intimidating but had to be done to accomplish God's direction for him. Trusting in God brought victory. The victory prepared him to be king.

From ages 17 to 30, he was running as a fugitive from jealous King Saul. He was learning the valuable lessons of total submission to God, while submitting to very poor leadership.

When David became 30 years old, he became King and ruled the kingdom. His lessons included walking in integrity and as a man after God's own heart. During these years he led well. David expanded Israel's borders from 6,000 to 60,000 square miles. He successfully led Israel's armies in war and expanded trade routes throughout the world bringing in wealth like never before. David unified Israel and created a powerful empire like no other.

When he moved into his later years, ages 50 to 70, he began a downhill slide as a broken man with a broken heart after sin with Bathsheba (2 Samuel 11:1–17).

David's Humanity: three major failures

➡ Became consumed with work and lost control of his family.

➡ Indulged in his passions of the flesh.

➡ A victim of pride.

In conclusion, David was an incredible man of God and a very successful leader who ruled well in his Leader season, but did not finish well in the later years of life

LESSONS TO LEARN:

➡ God does not qualify us by how we look or the diplomas on the wall.

➡ David was trained for all God used him for. His time tending sheep and fighting lions and bear made him a warrior. What are those lessons in your early years?

➡ He was ready to be king, and the works he accomplished were vast and skilled. Have you ever thought you were ready for something, but found out later, humbly maybe, that you were not?

➡ God clearly blessed David, but David allowed the world in and it happened fast. No one is immune to the works of the evil one, especially those who fight with and for Jesus. Where is Satan working on you, your tender spot? You must be aware of the places Satan seeks in your life and the sound of his voice.

 APPLICATION
10 minutes

The Leader season of a man's life is a time for action. All of your life experiences have prepared you for this time in your life. There is no room for passivity. You have learned from the good and the bad. You have made the mistakes of your youth and you must now lead with confidence. This season will be your most influential, with other people looking to you to lead them. Lead them well. Lead them like Jesus led his followers, with extreme love and grace and by example.

Jesus modeled the most radical of leadership styles: servant leadership. He said, "*The greatest among you are those who serve.*" He modeled it by getting on His knees and washing His disciples' feet on their last night together. People are drawn to love and humility—that is the Jesus way.

If you are a younger man, find a leader you can walk with and learn under. It is a critical piece of your life training to find these men. Watch how they live their lives, treat others, build and manage their kingdoms. It is an ancient path all men need to understand as they move forward, and you can only get it from another man.

CLOSING QUESTION
5 minutes

Has God placed you as the head of your family, a leader at work, or in a ministry? What are the qualities you have seen in the men you admire who are leaders? Describe them and things you do or might do to model them.

ACTION STEPS

Take a day and fast. Spend the day in prayer and quiet. Ask Jesus, "Am I a faithful steward of all I have? Do I tithe well?"

Ask Him: "Am I engaged where you want me or am I avoiding Your calling?"

Pray: "Jesus, my heart longs to be the man of God you are calling me to be. Lord, place me with other men who have walked these uneven grounds before me. Help me to see what it is you have for me."

CLOSING PRAYER

Father,

I thank you for everything both good and bad that has happened to me in my lifetime that has prepared me for this season of my life. Many lessons are learned more effectively in the storms of life, and You have always been there for me to get me through them and help me learn from them. I am ready to lead my family and my co-workers and my ministry partners well.

I thank You for the lessons of the great men of faith like David, but most of all for the example of Your son Jesus.

But God demonstrates his own love for us in this: While we were still sinners, Christ died for us. Romans 5:8

To know that I am loved by the Father, Son, and Holy Spirit in spite of my sin and shortcomings inspires me to love like You love unconditionally and with great passion.

I accept my responsibility to lead and to love during this season of my life. Amen

Chapter 6
SETTLING IN WISDOM
(60s forward)

Getting old does not seem old when you are in it. Yes, your bones may creak a bit, you move a bit slower, and you might watch what you eat a bit more. It can also be the best time of your life. By this time, you should have taken enough hits to know how to avoid them again. You talk less, listen more. Think before you act. Love on your kids and really love on your grandkids. This should be a wonderful time with God, family, and friends.

The Wisdom season is the final stage where a man has raised his children, completed most of his big work tasks, and is a wealth of information. It is not a point where he sits in his chair waiting to die. This can be the best stage of life. In this fourth quarter, the trail begins to wind down to basecamp and is overflowing with opportunities. He should be ready to enjoy the fruit of his labors. He loves his grandkids and can be a huge influence in their walk with Christ. He also enjoys quiet times and the freedom of the empty nest. He has the ability to pour into others his years of courage, strength, wisdom, and brokenness. He is mindful—his words are fewer but more thought out and intentional. He can be an example as he walks in his relationship with Christ. This may be the most important time of a man's life. He desperately wants to be remembered as leaving a good and Godly legacy. God has much for the man in the Wisdom season to do and it is critical.

ENDING THIS QUARTER WELL

| TJ |

As I sit here and write this, my son and daughter-in-law just gave us our first grandchild. A girl, Saylor. My daughter Taylor is planning her marriage and my youngest Jon-Michael is out on his own. My heart is tender. The kids are gone and we had not had a baby in the family for over 20 years. Joe Don told me that this was going to be a game changer. It did. It is.

So I am headed into the end of the third quarter of this life. I am not yet in the Wisdom mode, but my thoughts are changing about what the future looks like. Friends and family are older, some are dying. I can find myself thinking, "Did my life matter? Have I made a difference somewhere? Was I a good husband, dad, and friend? Will I be able to care for the things I need to as we get older? Will I finish strong?"

His master replied, 'Well done, good and faithful servant! You have been faithful with a few things; I will put you in charge of many things. Come and share your master's happiness!' Mathew 25:23

I have a lot left to do—mountains to climb, work for Jesus. I am not done, but I want to know the way ahead. I am blessed to have a man walking ahead of me, teaching me how to navigate what is to come. For that I am grateful. Thank you, Jesus, for fathering me in all the ways of my heart. Thank you, Joe Don, for riding this trail faithfully with me. So often I did not deserve forgiveness and kindness, but you offered it anyway. You shepherd me in areas I did not know I needed. Thank you, Papa Joe.

THE WISDOM SEASON

| JOE DON |

I looked in the mirror one day and I saw my Grandpa. What happened? It seems like only a short time ago I was standing on a mountain outside of Denver saying "I do" to the question, "Do you take Joann to be your wife and promise to love and cherish her for the rest of your life?" The memories of raising our family together bring a smile to my face.

I reflect back over the years after I trusted Christ and how everything changed for the better. My early years were filled with working hard and studying to become a pastor, with the victories, failures, and incredible memories of seeing God's Kingdom advanced. I learned how to love others and to battle the enemy. I grew as a leader and saw results far beyond what I could ever have imagined.

I have grown older now. My hair is gray and my face is full of wrinkles with stories behind each one. I ponder the past memories—preaching weekly, leading a staff, people looking to me for counsel in their marriages and life. But alas, I have finally entered the last season of life. I am now a Sage.

Once again, I have to learn new things. I wish my dad had not died when I was a little boy. I could have used the wisdom of watching how he navigated this challenging season.

I chose a Bible mentor early on in my walk—an Old Testament leader to model my life after. As a young man, I chose to model my life after Caleb. He was a mighty man of God as a young man and a mighty man of God as an old man. I wanted to be like Caleb then, and I will have my chance now as I grow older and still want to serve God wholeheartedly. As a Sage I will be an influencer of the next generation. My experience and wisdom accumulated along the way will now be my greatest asset.

I will be a Yoda to Luke or maybe a Gandalf who inspires all the young leaders and warriors in The Lord of the Rings. The wise one who has survived the battles and lived to tell the stories. One who can impart wisdom to help the younger ones be victorious in life and ministry.

I want to finish strong like Caleb who volunteered at the age of 85 to lead the battle in the taking of the final town in the conquest for the Promised Land.

I will not go quietly into the night, but will live out my life filled with passion for God, my family, and the legacy I leave behind.

More Stories
Along the Wisdom Path

LEGACY

| JOE DON |

What kind of old person do I want to be? Read Joshua 14:7–14.

So let me begin by asking you a question... What kind of old person do you want to be?

I know that most of you are young and you have not given a moment of thought about what you will be like when you are old. I understand completely, but it is a very important question that you must ask yourself. The type of old person you will be is determined by what kind of young person you are today.

Legacy is what we leave behind. Our legacy will be determined by whether our life really mattered. Each one of us has an opportunity to influence the next generation. Our lives today can inspire our children, our grandchildren, and even our great grandchildren to live their lives differently.

Every one of us can leave a spiritual legacy that will live on. The message of the Bible is that every life matters. We have been given the gift of life and most of us have received the gift of eternal life. The question is whether our lives will inspire others to follow in our footsteps. Will others choose Christ by our life example?

The date was January 16, 2000. My son was a college basketball player in California and his team was playing North Texas. Joann and I had traveled from Denver, Colorado, to Denton, Texas, to watch the game.

Here is my journal entry for that day in my life:

I am sitting in the lobby of a hotel in Denton, Texas, waiting for my son to come down. They are catching an early flight back to California after playing a game last night.

I am reflecting back on his life; he is now 20, soon to be 21.

To me he is still a little boy. The only thing that has changed is that his body has grown. It has grown a lot. But to me, his Dad, I still look at him as a little boy.

He just came down and walked out of the elevator. He looked so grown up.

We talked for a brief moment, we hugged and told each other how much we loved each other, and then he walked out of the doors of the hotel.

As he walked out, I realized for the first time that he was no longer a little boy; he was now a man.

Tears came to my eyes as I began to wonder. I hope I've instilled in him what's really important. To love God, to love his family, to be as gentle as a shepherd, and a fierce warrior against the kingdom of darkness.

Have I passed the baton to him? Have I shown him how to run the race of life? When he stumbles and falls will he get up? How will he respond when he's tempted? Will he say no and run? When he's tempted to quit, will he persevere? When being a Christian is tough, will he give up? When his marriage is challenging, will he stand strong and stay?

I sit alone in an empty lobby in a hotel, far away from home with tears running down my cheeks and hope that I have touched my son's soul.

♥ YOUR HEART TRAIL ♥

You want to live a life with no regrets. What are the values you hope to instill in your sons and daughters and grandsons and granddaughters? You must decide as a younger man and do the work necessary. It won't just happen. Do it now and enjoy the fruits of your efforts during your Sage season of life. Resolve today to live a life with no regrets.

What things would you want to be remembered most for if you left this life today?

_____

_____

_____

_____

_____

_____

_____

_____

_____

_____

_____

We will not hide them from their children, but tell to the coming generation the glorious deeds of the Lord, and his might, and the wonders that he has done. Psalm 78:4

For I am already being poured out as a drink offering, and the time of my departure has come. I have fought the good fight, I have finished the race, I have kept the faith. Henceforth there is laid up for me the crown of righteousness, which the Lord, the righteous judge, will award to me on that Day, and not only to me but also to all who have loved his appearing. 2 Timothy 4:6–8

CHAPTER 6
BIBLE STUDY

OPENING DISCUSSION
QUESTIONS *15 minutes*

Go around the circle and have the men answer one of these questions:

➡ What part of the Heart Trail spoke to you?

➡ Have you watched someone navigate their later years? What did they do well? Where did they go wrong?

➡ Have you ever had a moment with Jesus where you realized something and it brought you to tears?

LEADER: So many emotions can be found in the study this week on legacy, the final chapters of someone's life and what it means. It is important not to allow fear to guide your emotions when you are considering this season of life.

The world tells us that legacy is about how much stuff you can pass down, your name on a library, or cash in the bank. It is not.

> *Billy Graham said,* **"The greatest legacy one can pass on to one's children and grandchildren is not money or other material things accumulated in one's life, but rather a legacy of character and faith."**

If we knew it was our last days, we would most likely forget about our Facebook profile and emails. Our gun collections and new truck would not be what we want to spend time with. It would be family, friends, and loved ones. But we have to be intentional about how we prepare and how we navigate this incredibly important time.

BIBLE STUDY
25 minutes

What kind of old person do I want to be?

LEADER: There are no two greater goals in life than to live as a man of faith and to lead and love your family well. Legacy is what you leave behind. Caleb left a financial inheritance for his family in the land of Hebron. More importantly, Caleb left a spiritual inheritance of faith for his family. In both passages above, the characteristic of both Caleb as a young man and an old man was that "he followed the Lord, the God of Israel, wholeheartedly." He was an extremely passionate man, especially in his love for God and his family.

STUDY OF CALEB

Take turns reading out loud.

Caleb as a young man

I was forty years old when Moses the servant of the Lord sent me to explore the land. And I brought him back a report according to my convictions, but my brothers who went up with me made the hearts of the people melt with fear. I, however, followed the LORD my God wholeheartedly. So on that day Moses swore to me, 'The land on which your feet have walked will be your inheritance and that of your children forever, because you have followed the LORD my God wholeheartedly. Joshua 14:7–8

Caleb as a young man was a man of action and decisiveness. He was brave and courageous and advised Moses to take the Promised Land. He and Joshua were outvoted ten to two, and as a result the nation of Israel would wander in the desert for forty years.

Caleb as an old man

Now then, just as the Lord promised, He has kept me alive for 45 years since the time He said this to Moses, while Israel moved about in the desert. So here I am today, 85 years old! I am still as strong today as the day Moses sent me out; I'm just as vigorous to go out to battle now as I was then. Then Joshua blessed Caleb and gave him Hebron as his inheritance. So Hebron has belonged to Caleb ever since, because he followed the Lord, the God of Israel, wholeheartedly. Joshua 14:10–14

Forty-five years later at the age of 85, he was still as strong and vigorous as he was at 40. Although he was at the Sage stage of life, he was still a formidable warrior and was given the challenge of winning the last battle for the Promised Land. He was not retired but still involved in the advancement of God's Kingdom.

LEADER: Caleb was a man of great faith. Caleb was a man who loved his family well.

 APPLICATION
10 minutes

LEADER: It is very important to have a man of the wisdom stage in your life. A man of this season is older and wiser than you. A man of wisdom may come to you in many forms. He may be a car mechanic, a carpenter, or a hunter and he will help guide your steps in a Biblical way. He can teach you and help you go deeper and closer to God through the wisdom he has accumulated on his own personal journey with God.

He may be hard to find but you must pursue him. You must not go alone on the path of life. If your father is a man of God, then he is God's ordained mentor in your life, but unfortunately most men do not have such a treasure.

Our model is the Apostle Paul with young Timothy the pastor. Don't settle for a friend in the same season of life as yourself. Look for a man of God with gray hair and scars from the journey and lessons learned that he can teach you.

CLOSING CONVERSATION

Discuss among yourselves those who have such a mentor and the benefits. Talk about what legacy you were left by your parents or others. Finally, what legacy are you going to leave your family?

ACTION STEPS

Do you need to meet with an older man, a grandfather, or other man to whom you owe a debt of gratitude? What about someone to whom you need to make amends? Write a letter to them if you can't meet or if they have passed away.

Pursue a Mentor wholeheartedly and submit yourself to his wise counsel. This has been a theme throughout this study. Talk about legacy.

If you are a Mentor, be available to mentor a younger man in the ways of God. Men desperately desire time with older men and often don't know it.

Write out what it is you want to leave behind. Write about your heart not your stuff.

CLOSING PRAYER

Father, I need You most of all in this last season of my life. I thank You for all of the life lessons You have taught me. Throughout all of the tough times in life, You have walked with me and taught me along the way. I make myself available to young men who need my counsel. Speak to me the wisdom I can impart to them.

(For younger men) Father, show me the Sage You have for me, both living and dead (like Caleb). Help me find them. Develop in me the heat of a Sage, so when I grow old, I too can mentor younger men.

I love my family, Lord, and want to leave a Godly Legacy. Help me, Lord, to pass on the faith to my children and my children's children. Make me a man of God that they want follow. Amen

Chapter 7
DESTINY IN AN ENCOUNTER WITH JESUS

BIBLE STUDY

| JOE DON |

LEADER: So now as we finish up this study, there is one final thought to rally around. Can God really use me? I am so ordinary and have so many flaws. Can God use even me?

You have been on a seven-week journey seeking God's will for your life, and hopefully you have seen how God has used two very ordinary men (TJ & Joe Don) with a whole lot of flaws to do amazing things in them and thru them. You have read their stories and walked alongside of their hardships and stumbles along the path of life.

But there is one last story you must read!

GROUP: *Go around the room and have each guy read a piece of John 21:1–19*

LEADER: *(read this to men and stop along the way to add your comments)*

You just read TJ's favorite story in all of the Bible and you see how Jesus changes a man's destiny in one last encounter with Peter. Both TJ and I have had similar encounters with Jesus and will testify that you too can experience a complete life change if you are only willing to believe. To believe not just in Jesus, but in yourself.

Let's take this one last story and let Jesus change you, like he changed Peter and two Texas boys.

Peter wore a sign on his heart that read, "Gone fishing. Be back later—maybe."

Peter had hit rock bottom and felt so bad in himself. How could he have let Jesus down when He needed him the most? He had screwed up so badly.

He remembered telling Jesus, no matter what, I won't let You down. Others may, but not me. You can count on me. I am Peter and I am bold and brash.

Peter remembered Jesus responded with a story about a chicken crowing and how he would betray Him before the rooster crowed three times.

The bad news is Peter did disown Jesus. He denied even knowing Jesus although they had spent the last three years together walking the countryside and eating together and talking around a campfire at night and loving each other and seeing incredible miracles on an almost daily basis.

How could I ever have done such a thing to my friend, my Savior, my Lord?

I am a complete failure as a "fisher of men" that Jesus called me. So I am checking out and going back to what I know. Fishing for fish. Gone fishing. Be back later—maybe.

The good news is Jesus never disowned Peter.

He sought Peter out and knew Peter's favorite fishing spot and went there one morning early and started a campfire knowing Peter would be tired and hungry after a whole night of fishing.

Nothing better than fresh fish cooked on an open fire. Peter's favorite meal.

Here comes Peter worn out from trying all night to catch some fish and had caught none. He felt like an even bigger loser now. "I can't even catch fish, much less men like Jesus believed I could."

But from the shore a familiar voice says:

"Throw your net on the right side of the boat and you will find some."
When they did, they were unable to haul the net in because of the
large number of fish. John 21:6

What? No one can work a miracle like that…except Jesus.

Then the disciple whom Jesus loved said to Peter, "It is the Lord!" As
soon as Simon Peter heard him say, "It is the Lord," he wrapped his
outer garment around him (for he had taken it off) and jumped into
the water. The other disciples followed in the boat, towing the net
full of fish, for they were not far from shore, about a hundred yards.
When they landed, they saw a fire of burning coals there with fish on
it, and some bread. John 21:7–9

Peter had one last encounter with Jesus that changed his life forever.

Jesus wasn't mad or disappointed. He always believed in Peter, even when Peter did not believe in himself.

He didn't scold Peter. Jesus simply asked him three questions:

"Do you love me Peter?" Not once, not twice, but three times. The same number of times Peter denied Jesus.

Each time Peter responded back, "Yes, Lord You know I love You."

That was all Jesus needed to know.

If you love Me Peter, then "feed My sheep."

So Peter's story is just like TJ's and my story and your story.

Jesus extends to us grace we do not deserve and forgiveness even when we know Him and still sin against Him.

The last question to be answered is do you believe God can use you?

If you still doubt after seven weeks of studying the lives of three very ordinary men named TJ and Joe Don and Peter, then you are like a guy who doubted too. His name was Thomas and to this day he is referred to as Doubting Thomas.

But Jesus loved him as well and even used him too.

The truth is you have no excuses.

Believe in Jesus and believe that He can use even you. Yes, even you.

Your whole destiny can be changed with just one more encounter with Jesus.

CHAPTER 7
 BIBLE DISCUSSION

A story of God doing great things through ordinary guys.

LEADER: *Go around the room and ask each guy this question:*

How are you like Peter? Where do you cast Jesus aside most often? Your work, with your wife or kids, while out with your buddies, or maybe online?

_____

_____

_____

_____

_____

Are you willing to be used by God to do great things? What are some things you might be interested in praying about? What are some new things you can commit to as you step into a mission for Jesus? A ministry, a task at church, a Bible study, or something with your wife?

_____

_____

_____

_____

_____

What is keeping you from fully giving your will, your life, your destiny to Jesus? Fear, money, lack of time, agreements with yourself that don't belong there anymore. (Talk about it and write down your thoughts.)

CONCLUDING THIS TIME TOGETHER AT BASE CAMP

LEADER: *Read this to your men:*

From TJ & Joe Don: So, if you are reading this you are at the end of the book. Congratulations—job well done. The reason we wrote this was because we were amazed at what God did with us. We, to this day, are in awe of how he took the pieces we thought were broken and unusable and tooled them into something for His Kingdom. We wanted to share the trail from when we were boys to today. We wanted you to know that you matter, you have what it takes. God chose you from before you were conceived to this very day for something that only you are here to do.

So what is it? What has he said to you the last few weeks? Look back at your notes — is it getting clear? If you feel you are operating in His Kingdom, did He reveal things that are keeping you from clarity or moving forward? Did He use it to enhance your gifts or testimony?

Every man must have a mission. Not a simple task, but one that creates blisters, blood, and scrapes for the gospel. Your heart longs for it, your soul needs it, every man does.

If you are not sure, stay in prayer. Ask Him, "Jesus what is it you have for me?"

**The last question to be asked is,
"Do you believe God can use you?"**

LEADER: So guys, as we finish this week, we should think about what we can do from here? Do you want to build on this men's ministry opportunity?

It is important to build on the closeness you have in your group. There are several ways to do this. One is to continue meeting each week. This is powerful and you will be amazed at what continues to happen. You have momentum on your side.

Suggestions for your group time are:

➡ A Bible study. A book of the Bible.

➡ Bare Bones Bible by Jim George is great. One chapter per week.

➡ A men's ministry book study. (*Wild at Heart* by John Eldredge is a great next step.)

➡ Tool Box: Study a different topic each week for several weeks. Fear, Loss, Giving, Marriage, Love, Kids. Assign a couple of guys each to bring a piece to teach each week.

➡ Testimony Tuesdays: Invite in a different man from the community who knows Jesus to come share his testimony. Do this with several men for several weeks. Then pray over him at the end.

➡ For more of Base Camp Men's Ministry go to BaseCampMensMinistry.com.

Guidelines for the Base Camp Men's Ministry Meeting
THE BASE CAMP BASIC TOOL BOX:

The original Base Camp Men's Group includes much of the above. They have met with a group of committed guys on Tuesday night for years. They have seen lots of guys come and go. One thing they hear from the men even years after they leave is that they have never been in a more real, man-friendly men's group. Their time at Base Camp was transformational in their lives.

Some weeks they will have guys from ten to twelve different churches. They don't focus on just one church—it's all different churches! They include a meal each week provided by one of the men. They build a fire in the fire pit and hang out before they start. They also have lots of guys who smoke cigars or pipes around the campfire as they fellowship. It is real men pursuing Jesus in real life with a band of brothers. A no judgment zone.

Five important things for a Base Camp:

➡ It is not church or Sunday school. Be real. Talk real.
   Accept real life, warts and all. True leaders share from their hearts.

➡ You are men. Push into what a real man is, how a real man needs to operate and live his life. Call BS when necessary.

➡ Go to Jesus in prayer often as a group of men. It does not have to be a pretty little prayer. Real, raw, from your heart, led by the Holy Spirit. Put a guy in the middle of the room and circle around him with hands on prayer when they need it. This is a fight so use the tools you were given by the King.

➡ Be Spirit led and not Old Testament laws and rules.

➡ Every guy is broken in some area of his life. Every guy! No matter the social level or religious level, all men are fighting something. When we humble ourselves and allow Jesus to work through the Holy Spirit, we change.

FINAL CONVERSATIONS

LEADER: In a beautiful and amazing moment Jesus came back and forgave Peter in John 21. It is one of the most powerful parts of the Bible.

All of the shame Peter ever imagined would go away. Jesus does that for us, all of us. Know you are forgiven if your heart belongs to Jesus, and He has a plan for you to do something astonishing.

Commit to spending the next week in prayer as a group and ask God what it is He wants you to do. Meet next week with food and fellowship, and talk through what each of you has heard. Know Satan is not happy with you guys. He wants to break you up. He does not want another army of men fighting against him.

If you are an existing KOZ group or men's ministry, take this time to fine tune your hearts together. Where is God taking you?

Jesus met with His men for the last time around a campfire. He met them where they knew Him best. Men, together. Don't go religious on your men. Love them as Jesus loved His men, and your group will do mighty things.

In closing, we want to thank all of the men who have walked alongside of us in this journey into manhood. Your stories have inspired us. You have proven that life change does happen in circles and not rows.

If we can ever help, please call. You guys matter to us.

Godspeed,
Joe Don Mayes. TJ Greaney. Friends.

FACILITATOR INSTRUCTIONS FOR GROUP BIBLE STUDIES

This 7-week study can be done individually or in a group. However, we recommend you do the study with a group of men. Men learn best from other men. We believe life transformation happens best in a circle rather than rows. Create an atmosphere of warmth and acceptance, but a man's atmosphere. A garage, cabin, barn, or room with animal heads on the wall work well. Do your best here but the more manly, the better. Don't just default into a classroom at church; find a guy's place or build one.

You are a facilitator and not a lecturer. This is not your normal Men's Bible Study where men sit and listen as the leader does all the talking. There will be moments you teach, but mostly you will ask questions and encourage discussion. Have men bring their Bibles and read from them when you reference Scripture.

During the week prior to the meeting time, each man should read the chapter, the stories, and answer the questions. (Please note that the reading before the first week's study will include the Introduction and Chapter 1.) This is their commitment to the study. Encourage each man to be ready to share his insights with the group.

You should be creating a group of men, Base Camp Men's Group. Giving the men a sense of being part of a unified group makes a big difference.

Open the meeting with prayer, surrendering yourself to God. Welcome God into the discussion and ask the Holy Spirit to speak directly to each man in the room. "Holy Spirit, help us learn the lessons from our previous and future paths of life in this walk with God."

How the night lays out:

HOURS: 6:30 to 8:30 pm are good.

FOOD: We have been very successful in taking turns bringing food for the group. Each guy signs up on a calendar. We hang out from 6:30 to 7:00. At 7:00 we rally together and begin eating. At about 7:15, start with announcements, then get the meeting started by 7:30.

OPENING DISCUSSION QUESTIONS
15 minutes

Talk about the stories that they read that week, beginning with the first one. Ask the guys what their takeaways were for the first one. Then go to the second one. Go around the circle and have each guy answer or read from his notes about one of the stories. (If the group is large, then allow only a few to speak.) This is your best tool to get each man involved. Be careful to not let one guy go long. There might be a guy with all the answers. Let them know each man needs a chance to share, so limit the time. You may have to step in here—you are the Leader.

BIBLE STUDY
25 minutes

The Leader will teach from the notes provided. Familiarize yourself with the text beforehand and involve men in reading the Scripture out loud and ask questions along the way to facilitate discussion. Remember this is not a lecture but a discussion. Men learn from other men as well as formulating their own opinions. Let the talk happen.

Consider having different guys read a section.

Application: 10 minutes

This is when you process the study and apply it to your lives. Application is a must. Ask the questions and encourage participation. Tell personal stories if applicable. When you get real, your men will get real. The more real you are, the more real they will get.

CLOSING DISCUSSION QUESTION
5 minutes

The Leader reads the Action Steps and opens for questions and thoughts.

PRAYER
5 minutes

This is a great time to let different guys close in prayer. Who was engaged in the study, moved by the materials?

If there is a special need from a particular man, you may put him in the middle of the room, circle around him with hands on him, and pray over him. This is a powerful gesture by a group of men.

Remember our target is a man's heart and not his head. You can do this. Rely on the Holy Spirit to guide you. Men rarely have the chance to participate at this level. Usually they are talked to or talked at. If they participate in deep discussion, they begin to see value in their words, hearts, and experiences.

RESOURCES FOR GROWING STRONGER

READ:

Year 13: *A wounded boy's journey to manhood and ministry* by TJ Greaney

Wild at Heart: *Discovering the Secret of a Man's Soul*, by John Eldredge

Fathered by God: *Learning What Your Dad Could Never Teach You*, by John Eldredge

Raising a Modern-Day Knight: *A Father's Role in Guiding His Son to Authentic Manhood*, by Robert Lewis

Making Men: *Five Steps to Growing Up*, by Chuck Holton

GO:

To a Wild at Heart Boot Camp or do a Basic Boot Camp from
Wild at Heart Ministry www.WildatHeart.org.
Do it completely with no short cuts.

START A KIDS OUTDOOR ZONE (KOZ) GROUP:

Every man needs a mission. Something bigger than himself. This is key to living a life alive in the Holy Spirit. KOZ will open the door to your heart. There are boys out there waiting desperately for a man to be there for them. You offer the eternal gift of salvation for a fatherless boy and his soul. Your sons will be moved in a poignant and powerful way.

Made in the USA
Las Vegas, NV
13 May 2024

89887752R00070